Unlocking the Secrets of Hanuman Chalisa

A verse-by-verse interpretation

OrangeBooks Publication

1st Floor, Rajhans Arcade, Mall Road, Kohka, Bhilai, Chhattisgarh 490020
Website: **www.orangebooks.in**

First Edition, 2025

ISBN: 978-93-6554-505-0

Price: Rs. 220.00

The opinions/ contents expressed in this book are solely of the author and do not represent the opinions/ standings/ thoughts of Orange Books.

Printed in India

UNLOCKING THE SECRETS OF HANUMAN CHALISA

A VERSE-BY-VERSE INTERPRETATION

TANMAY PADHI

OrangeBooks Publication
www.orangebooks.in

Dedicated to

Sri Hanuman ji

Late Baba Rampyari Das Maharaj

Late Dr Biranchi Narayana Padhi

PREFACE

My association with Lord Hanuman goes back to the days when I had not even started going to school. Maharaj, as we would fondly and respectfully call him, was the one who introduced me and my brother to the world of Hanuman. Baba Rampyari Das "Maharaj" of Bilaspur, Chhattisgarh, was not just a spiritual Guru; he was divinity personified for thousands of his devotees.

The thought that the verses of an apparently simple text such as the *Hanuman Chalisa* need further explanation had not occurred to me till recently. The works of several authors and speakers on the *Chalisa* have come up in the last few years, thanks to the spread of the internet. I became aware of my ignorance about the literal meaning of the *Chalisa* verses only after going through them. And gradually, my interest in finding the deeper meaning grew. About three years back, I came across the famous *Mahaviri Vyakhya* in Hindi by Jagadguru Swami Sri Rambhadracharya ji. Swamiji's authoritative explanation of the text is a must-read for scholars as well as all the devotees of Sri Hanuman. This text has been translated and further expanded into English by Sri Nityananda Misra. My thoughts on writing something on the *Chalisa* took a solid form when I went through the *Mahaviri Vyakhya*.

Very few commentaries or even expanded translations exist on the Hanuman Chalisa. This is surprising, given the immense popularity of the cult of Hanuman and also of the text of the Hanuman Chalisa. This book is a modest attempt to fill the gap.

With all my humility, I admit that I am not a scholar of Awadhi or Hindi literature. This book is a product of pure enthusiasm. Though I have taken due care to present the facts correctly, I never mean to be absolutely accurate in their interpretation. The Hanuman Chalisa is a song of pure devotion, and no one can dispute that ever. However, like many other timeless compositions of the *Sanatan parampara*, it does contain glimpses of multiple philosophies. I have tried to look at the *Chalisa* from that angle.

Moreover, there is a pattern of thought not only in the arrangement of the verses but also in the positioning of words within a single verse. I have tried to reconstruct that pattern while exploring the meanings of the verses.

Many of the verses in the *Chalisa* relate to events from the Ramayana or to specific attributes of Hanuman. During recitation, the average reader does understand this relationship, but he is mostly ignorant of the details. More importantly, the background events or attributes do not exclusively belong to the *Ramcharitmanas*. The Vedas, Puranas, different versions of the Ramayana, and other books authored by Tulsidas have all been the source materials for the Hanuman Chalisa. Within this short work, I have tried to recall those ancient and medieval references that form the background of the *Chalisa* verses.

During the process of writing this book, I have borrowed ideas and facts from several works. Principal among them are the *Mahaviri Vyakhya* of Swami Rambhadracharyaji, *Hanuman* by Catherine Ludvik, and *Hanuman's Tale: The Messages of a Divine Monkey* by Philip Lutgendorf. Then, there are Hindi and English translations of the works of Tulsidas, Krittivasa Ramayana, Kamban Ramayana, Adhyatma Ramayana, Vyasa Mahabharata, Rig Veda, Agastya Samhita, and so on. I thank the authors and publishers of all these works from the core of my heart.

Finally, I express my thanks and gratitude to Pankajini Padhi, my mother; Dr Pranamita, my wife; Aprameyaa, my daughter; and Chinmaya, my elder brother, for all their love, support and encouragement during the publication of this book.

ॐ

Contents

ॐ

INTRODUCTION

Millions of Hindus begin their day with a prayer to Lord Hanuman. Along with the sacred *Gayatri mantra* and the very famous *Venkatesha Suprabhatam*, the *Hanuman Chalisa* can easily be considered as the most frequently recited morning prayer across India. That Hanuman ji is one of the most loved deities is attested by His ubiquitous presence: from car dashboards to interiors of gyms and from temple entrances in remote villages to puja rooms of modern apartments. The popularity of the *Chalisa* verses has followed a similar trajectory. One can find them as a background score not only in children's movies and cartoon shows, but also in mainstream Bollywood movies and the hugely popular Hindi soap operas.

The Valmiki Ramayana, composed a few centuries before the common era, had already established Hanuman as a household name across the subcontinent and even beyond. Archaeological surveys have found His statues belonging to the 3rd and 4th centuries of the first millennium. However, the second resurgence of the *Hanuman wave* can be traced to the medieval period. The royal patronage of the Vijayanagara and the Maratha Empires firmly established the cult of Anjaneya across peninsular India. In the northern plains, His immense popularity owes its origin to the timeless works of Tulsidas.

The Poet

As with many Indian saints and saint-poets of the medieval period, Tulsidas's life story is shrouded in mystery. Following the prevailing tradition, the poet himself has not divulged much about his personal journey. The year of his birth and death, the place of his birth, and even his marital status have all been matters of debate. The years of his birth have been variously suggested as 1497, 1511, 1532 and 1543 CE. Similarly, three villages have been proposed as the place of his birth – Rajapur near Gonda, Uttar Pradesh; Rajapur near Chitrakoot; and Soro in Uttar Pradesh.

Originally named Rambola Dubey, the poet lived in and around Chitrakoot, Ayodhya and Varanasi, and most of his works have been composed in these places. Numerous legends and stories have treated him as a contemporary of Akbar, the Mughal emperor. The year of his death has more or less been accepted as 1623 CE.

Tulsidas was also known as Goswami ji, a title often used for Vaishnava saints. He was a disciple of Acharya Narahari Das, who belonged to the *Ramanandi* sect of Vaishnava saints. Organisations like the Sanatan Dharm Parishad and saints like Swami Rambhadracharya strongly believe that the poet was never married, as attested by his own writing in the *Vinay Patrika* and *Kavitavali.*

Some scholars have expressed their doubts about the Hanuman Chalisa being an authentic Tulsidas composition. The *Chalisa* does not find a place in the list of his works suggested by his biographers, and all the manuscripts of this text belong to a period after the eighteenth century. Some believe it to be the work of another Vaishnava saint, also named Tulsidas. However, the unmistakable style of Goswami ji can be seen in the structure of the poetry, selection of words, and sentiment of expression. Many of the themes, such as Sri Rama declaring Hanuman to be as dear to Him as Bharata, Hanuman carrying the signet ring of Rama within His mouth, and terms such as *Shankara suvana*, *mana-krama-vachana*, *amita jivana-phala,* bear the literary signature of Tulsidas.

Background

Historical and social context should always be considered when making sense of any text. There are two major theories, primarily based on legends, on when and why Goswami ji composed the *Chalisa*. The popular view says that he composed it when Akbar had put him in prison for not being able to show any miracle in his royal court. Tulsidas composed the verses to seek divine intervention, and lo, thousands of monkeys descended on the city of Agra. The Mughal sultan felt sorry for his rude behaviour and freed the saint-poet from prison. As per the second view, he composed it during the Kumbh Mela in Haridwar; the verses came through him while he was in a deep state of meditation there.

Let us move beyond his personal reasons and look at the larger picture. By the second half of the sixteenth century, North-western India had already endured over three and a half centuries of subjugation under Turkish,

Afghan and Mughal rule. This phase of Indian history had witnessed three significant changes.

First, the age-old tradition of *vāda* and *samvāda* had been lost. The average Hindu's spiritual quest had largely been replaced by a complete surrender to the will of the Almighty. Secondly, the assimilative Sanatan social values had also taken a backseat against the onslaught of foreign rule, and centuries of repression had created rifts in the social structure. Even on the religious front, Hindus had started identifying themselves with their sects and sub-sects. Thirdly, the *Bhakti Parampara* had become the flavour of the season. It was a tradition started long ago by the Alwars and Nayanars in the southern states. With the continued support of legends like Ramanujacharya, Madhavacharya, Ramanand, Kabir and Guru Nanak Dev, it had literally flooded the Sanatan mindscape across the length and breadth of the country.

Tulsidas chose the path of *Bhakti* and resolved to keep the flicker of hope sustained through a brand of literature that would touch the commoners and the intelligentsia alike. The need of the hour was to reassure people and motivate them to be a little more patient. Against this background, the Hanuman Chalisa emerged as a prayer that was short yet powerful. Indians had always been considered a little other-worldly, more interested in the well-being of their soul after death. The *Chalisa* verses spoke of happiness not just in the afterlife, but of a fruitful life right here, in this world.

The *Chalisa* is undoubtedly an out-and-out *bhakti* text. The Vaishnava emotions, particularly those of the

Ramanandi sect, can be seen in each and every word of this prayer-song. However, the presence of multiple undertones within a single composition is the hallmark of many ancient Indian texts, and the Hanuman Chalisa is no exception. There are reasons to believe that the *Chalisa*, at its core, contains the philosophy of Samkhya and Yoga. The careful reader may even find a glimpse of Advaita in the text. The mention of *mana-mukura* or the mind as a mirror is indirectly suggestive of a Samkhya influence. Similarly, yogic expressions like *siddhi* and *dhyana* frequently occur within this short text. And yet again, the poet of the *Chalisa* does not talk of *moksha or kaivalya,* the ultimate goal of the Samkhya-Yoga school. There is only an indirect reference to *moksha* in the first *doha*; rather, reincarnation as a *bhakta* has been mentioned in one of the verses. All these make the *Chalisa* a composite text that spreads the essence of multiple spiritual sentiments.

The *Ramanandi sampradaya* has a long history of respecting the views of Natha Yogis, even though the latter are considered *Shaivas*. The sect has produced saints of all kinds – wandering monks, warriors, poets and social reformers. No wonder the hallmark of Goswamiji's writing is the element of assimilation and integration. As Philip Lutgendorf has observed, "The *Ramcharitmanas* may seem to be conservative and hierarchy-affirming in letter, but it is inclusive and hierarchy-challenging in spirit."

Tulsidas has maintained his characteristic *Vaishnava–Shaiva samanvaya* in the verses of the *Chalisa*. This speaks about his unflinching devotion to both Hari and

Hara. But he did not do this just because of his *Ramanandi* credentials; it was the need of the hour. Opposition among the various sects of Hinduism, particularly between Vaishnavas and Shaivas, was well known. Tulsidas was one of the few torchbearers who strove hard to preserve the Sanatana Dharma as an ever-assimilating worldview. Hence, his Hanuman is a son of Mahadeva, and when he says that reciters of the *Chalisa* are assured of accomplishments in their lives, Gaurisha or Lord Shiva becomes the guarantor of the claim.

A short prayer of forty-three verses integrates seemingly opposing concepts like karma-jnana-bhakti, Vaishnava - Shaiva, masculine-feminine, human-divine, present life-after life, master-servant, and so on. The inquisitiveness of the *Jnana Parampara* has been integrated with the unconditional surrender of the *Bhakti tradition*. A prayer addressed to the *Divine* starts with invoking the blessings of a *Human Guru*. The verses glorify the eternal servant, but they also tell us that the servant is great because of an equally great master.

The *Ramcharitmanas* is not an Awadhi translation of Valmiki Ramayana or its abridged edition. It is an inspired text and, at the same time, a complete text in its own right. The meanings of the verses of the Hanuman Chalisa, as expected, are aligned more towards the Ramayana of Tulasi and other works of his, such as the *Vinay Patrika* and *Kavitavali*.

Valmiki has portrayed the character of Sri Hanuman differently. Valmiki's Hanuman is not only knowledgeable and powerful, He is also very human.

Like all of us, He gets confused, depressed, and even contemplates suicide. He is Rama's most trusted man. But the Hanuman of Tulsidas is above these limitations; He is supra-human. His bhakti for Raghuvara and Ma Sita is just out of this world. He Himself is the greatest bhakta and gets easily pleased when someone prays to Him with bhakti.

Structure:

The text of the Hanuman Chalisa has been presented as *Doha* and *Chaupai*. Both *Doha and Chaupai are based on Matrika chhanda,* which considers *matra* rather than *varna* or syllables.

A *doha* or couplet consists of two lines or four quarters – the first and third quarters contain 13 beats (*matra*) and the second and fourth have 11 beats each.

Chaupai or quatrain is identified by a *matra* count of 16 in each quarter. Short or *Hrasva* sounds are considered one *matra,* while long or *Dirgha* sounds or a short vowel followed by a consonant are counted as two *matras*.

Technically speaking, there are twenty and not forty *chaupais* in the *Chalisa*. However, each *chaupai* is taken as a combination of two verses. Therefore, we find forty-three verses in the text – three *dohas* as three verses and twenty *chaupais* as forty verses. The text is structured as two *dohas* in the beginning, followed by twenty *chaupais* and a concluding *doha* at the end.

Characters:

The prayer is addressed to Hanuman ji, so for all practical purposes, He is the protagonist here. And a considerable portion of the text is a eulogy to Lord Rama. Together, they form the bulk of the Hanuman Chalisa. The text also mentions Lakshmana and Sita, Lord Brahma, Lord Shiva, Yama, Kuvera, Shesha Naga, Narada, Sarasvati, mind-born sons of Lord Brahma like Sanaka and other characters of Ramayana like Sugreeva and Vibhishana.

Lastly, it carries an implicit reference to the Guru of the poet, Acharya Narahari Das and an explicit reference to Tulsidas ji, the poet himself.

The name Hanuman or Hanumat has been mentioned seven times within the text – four times as Hanuman and thrice as Hanumat. Hanuman's master, the greatest of the Raghu dynasty, scores even higher, and the name Rama has eleven mentions within these forty-three verses. One of these is a synonym of Hanuman ji (*Ram doot*), and even then, Sri Rama gets ten mentions to His credit. However, we must not forget that Hanuman ji has mostly been addressed with many of His epithets, such as *Kapisha, Mahavira, Pavana Tanaya, Anjani Putra, Shankara Suvana, Keshari Nandana,* and so on.

Content organization:

A close look at the sequence and meaning of the verses unfolds an underlying pattern in their arrangement in the Hanuman Chalisa. The very first *doha* speaks about a preparation for something higher, and that objective gets materialized in the concluding *chaupai* and *doha*. So, there is a linear flow of thoughts from the beginning to the end. Within this uninterrupted chain of thoughts, a pattern emerges.

How so? Well, let us try to find the big picture and its five major components.

The first part is the introduction, the two *dohas*. The first *doha* starts with *Guru Vandana* and the merits of narrating Sri Rama's story. The second *doha* is a prayer to Sri Hanuman, seeking strength, intelligence, knowledge and freedom from hardships and impurities.

The introductory part, or the first component of the *Chalisa,* deals with three statements from Goswami ji-

Q. How shall I proceed?

A. I shall start by cleansing my mind through my Guru's blessings.

Q. Why should I proceed?

A. I need to sing the purest fame of Sri Rama, as it bestows everything that one may ask for.

Q. What do I need to proceed?

A. To achieve this target, I need strength, intelligence and knowledge, as well as freedom from hardships and impurities.

The next twenty *chaupais* with their forty verses can be broadly classified into four sub-groups of ten verses each. All the four components carry different senses. The division is broad; they do not fall into four groups of exactly ten verses. However, a beautiful, uninterrupted pattern emerges if we analyse the sense that each sub-section carries.

The second component, consisting of the first ten verses, tries to build an image of Lord Hanuman, which we can contemplate or meditate upon. It speaks about Hanumanji's general attributes – His looks, deeds and parentage. It also tells us about His different *rupa* or forms that He assumes as per the need: the conventional auspicious and good-looking form, the *sukshma* or minute form, the terrible form, and so on. We get a broad idea of what He does for His master and devotees. The whole purpose of these ten verses is to portray a picture of the *Prabhu* to meditate upon, to make it known that He is the rarest combination of *karma jnana bhakti*, of brain and brawn, of high IQ and an equally high EQ.

In the third component, or the following ten verses, in fact, from the 9th verse itself, His exploits and extraordinary deeds have been narrated. The contents of this section deal with how He saved Lakshmana's life, found Sita, burnt down the city of Lanka, and finally killed the demons, all assuming different forms. A large part of the third component deals with three of His most popular aerial journeys. From the 11th to the 15th verse, Tulsidas speaks about Hanuman bringing the *Sanjivani* herb and Sri Rama's heartfelt gratitude towards Him. This five-verse-long description is the longest theme in the *Chalisa*. Rama embraces Him twice, gives Him the status of His brother Bharata, and proudly declares that all the divine entities, including celestials, sages, serpents, the Guardians of directions, men of knowledge, and even Lord Brahma and Goddess Sarasvati, can never speak about His greatness enough. The second half of this section, verses 16th to 20th, is all about how Hanuman had been a king-maker. Both Sugreeva and Vibhishana got their kingships, thanks to Anjaneya. The other two popular flights are mentioned here; they are popular because they had been executed effortlessly. Goswami ji hopes that with the blessings of Maruti, all such seemingly difficult tasks would become easy and effortless.

The fourth section, comprising of verses 21st to 30th, mostly speaks about the blessings and protection that a devotee receives from the Vayuputra. The poet has already expressed his desire for such benevolence in the introductory *dohas,* at the very beginning of the *Chalisa*. The path of self-realization is always full of surprises; we need a saviour of Maruti's stature to keep us protected. However, Goswami ji puts a condition that the devotee has to direct all his focus, mental, physical and verbal, towards the Lord. The fourth section also tells us that the purpose of Maruti's existence is to serve Raghupati.

The last section, which consists of verses 31st to 40th, is a mixed bag. The poet tells us how Hanuman holds the key to reaching Sri Rama, how praying to Him is the same as praying to His Master, and how His devotees get rid of all their sufferings. Tulsidas pleads Him to bless just as his human guru would do. He swears by the name of Mahadeva and proclaims that the reciter of the *Chalisa* would attain *siddhi* for sure. The poet ends the section by making a request to Hanumanji to reside within his heart.

And finally, he concludes with a *doha* with his one-point agenda of making his heart the abode of the Lords. This is the sole objective of the *Chalisa*.

Within what seems to be a random collection of forty-odd devotional verses, the pattern of thoughts has been organised somewhat like this:

A. An objective of having the Divine within our heart is set.

B. The appearance, forms and lineage of Hanuman are spoken of, through which we construct a mental image of Him and start meditating upon it.

C. His amazing acts, which won praise from Raghunatha Himself, are then narrated. Our devotion and trust in Him become rock solid.

D. The poet tells us that Maruti's blessings are enough to mitigate obstacles of any kind–disease, misfortune or an evil spirit. We gradually prepare and empower ourselves with His grace and start taking confident steps towards the goal.

E. And finally, Anjaneya takes us to the supreme goal irrespective of the path we follow – the Lords come to reside within us.

ॐ

SECTION I

The Introductory Dohas

श्रीगुरु चरन सरोज रज निज मनु मुकुरु सुधारि।
बरनउँ रघुबर बिमल जसु जो दायकु फल चारि॥

Having polished the mirror of my mind with dust from the lotus feet of my guru, I narrate the unblemished fame of Sri Rama that fulfils the four-fold goals of life.

This is the very first *doha* and, therefore, the introductory verse of the *Chalisa*. A superficial look at the words tells us that this is the typical beginning of a Hindu spiritual text. As per tradition, the blessing of the guru is sought at the very beginning. And because the *Chalisa* is a prayer to Hanuman ji, His master's name is mentioned before the prayer begins.

When we start reading it carefully, two questions come to mind. The first is, who is the "Shree Guru" here? The second question is a bit more complex: This is the beginning of a prayer to Hanuman ji; then, why does the poet say that he is going to narrate the fame of Sri Rama?

In real life, Narahari Das was the guru of the poet. He was the one who made Goswami ji well conversant with the Ramayana. The guru himself was a great poet in *Braj Bhasha*. Following the Vaishnava tradition, Tulsidas has invoked his blessings before proceeding to compose the verses. In the spiritual realm, however, he considered Hanuman ji as his guru. It was singularly the blessings of Maruti that led Goswami ji to become such a famous writer. Moreover, it was Maruti who led the poet to the sacred abode of Sri Rama. Even within this short text, he has not forgotten to address Hanumanji as *Gosai* (Goswami) and has prayed to Him to bless just like a guru would bless his disciple. So, "guru" here could be human, divine, or even both.

The *Mahaviri Vyakhya* has two opinions on the prefix *Shree* before guru. Here, *Shree* stands for Devi Sita, the symbol of eternal auspiciousness and prosperity. "Shree Guru" means either *Shree Herself as the guru* or *a guru who has the blessings of Shree*.

Mana-mukura, or the mind as a mirror, has been a recurring motif in Sanatan literature. It probably owes its origin to the Samkhya tradition. The external objects get reflected in the mind through the senses, but the supreme objective of life is to be able to see the reflection of the pure consciousness or soul, also known as the *Purusha*, in the mirror of the mind. And the mirror needs to be spotlessly clean to receive the reflection. The soul is the one with consciousness; it has its own light. The mind belongs to *Prakriti* and is devoid of any such attributes. Light from the soul has to fall on the mind, and then only the mind can see things as they are and not as they appear. While the Samkhya philosophy prescribes self-realization or *atma jnana,* for this cleansing act, Tulsidas seeks the blessings of his guru to make this happen.

If "mind" and "heart" can be used interchangeably, the poet has a great purpose in polishing his mind-slate at the very beginning. The objective is implicitly stated here – to have Hanuman ji, along with Their Holinesses

Sri Rama, Lakshmana and Sita, within his heart. The entire effort is being directed towards that goal.

Therefore, the song begins with cleaning the place in the first *doha,* and ends in the fortieth verse and the concluding *doha,* with a prayer to make this place their habitat. The mind can be cleansed through the control of the senses. As that is something very difficult to achieve, a guru's guidance is needed. When the *Devas* reside within us and we become aware of their existence, the four-fold desires get fulfilled, and nothing more remains to be achieved. This spiritual aspiration can be sensed at the very beginning of the *Chalisa,* and it has been mentioned twice more in the last verse. And for this aspiration to materialize, the blessings of *Adi Shakti* (*Prakriti*) and the Guru are essential.

Let us come to the second question – why is the poet keen on singing Rama's praise in the Hanuman Chalisa? The *Mahaviri Vyakhya* says that Hanuman ji does not accept His existence without a mention of Sri Rama. Secondly, Vaishnavas do not like their own praise to be sung. So, when a *Rama-bhakta* and a *Parama Vaishnava* like Anjaneya is the protagonist, the poet could not have composed otherwise.

But the most astonishing fact about the very first *doha* is that it is also the opening *doha* of the *Ayodhya Kanda* of *Ramcharitmanas*. After four shlokas in Sanskrit as *mangalacharan*, this verse in Awadhi is considered the beginning of the second *kanda* of Tulasi Ramayana. Keeping Rama at the beginning of *Ayodhya Kanda* looks appropriate, but how can the same verse be used as an introduction to the Hanuman Chalisa? *Ayodhya Kanda* does not deal with the character of Hanuman. However, styling the text of the Hanuman Chalisa as a praise-song of *the unblemished fame of the greatest of the Raghu dynasty* cannot be a random act. It has to have a specific purpose.

Vimala Rama Yasha is the bestower of *Phala chari,* or all four kinds of achievements. These have conventionally been interpreted as *Dharma, Artha, Kama* and *Moksha*. Some also relate them to the four kinds of liberations or *mukti* of the *Bhakti marga,* which are *Salokya*, *Samipya*, *Sarupya* and *Sayujya*.

A poorly substantiated theory claims that a devotee, also known as Tulsidas, copied the first verse of *Ayodhya Kanda* and wrote it at the beginning of the *Chalisa* manuscript, and hence, the confusion was created.

But no one knows Maruti better than Goswami ji. He wants to please the Lord, and there is only one way to achieve that – singing the praise of Sri Rama. Verses sung in His own praise are of no interest to Maruti unless the devotee says, "O Lord, I am singing the greatness of Raghunatha." As Philip Lutgendorf would say, "Maruti is the bearer of both Rama's ring and His story".

The poet lays down the true purpose of the text in the very first *doha* itself: to achieve self-realization through *Bhakti* and *Guru kripa*.

बुद्धिहीन तनु जानिके, सुमिरौं पवन कुमार।
बल बुधि विद्या देहु मोहि, हरहु कलेश विकार॥

Realising myself (my body) to be bereft of intelligence, I remember the Son of the Wind God. O Lord, bless me with strength, intelligence and knowledge, and take away my sufferings and deformities.

Tulsidas climbs a step above and moves from the mind to the intelligence. *Buddhi* or intelligence is the representative of the self or the soul within this body. Now that *manas,* or the mind, has been cleansed, *buddhi* can facilitate a meeting of it with the soul. Along with *buddhi*, the poet also asks for *bala* and *vidya*.

From a more real-life perspective, human intelligence is never fully capable of guiding us through difficult times. It loses its power of discrimination under pressure. Lord Hanuman is *buddhimatam varistham*, the greatest among the intelligent ones. Who else is better qualified to bless the devotee with a resolute intelligence than *Pavana Kumara*!

But, having *buddhi* alone is not enough to survive in this world; we must have strength and knowledge. *Vidya* or knowledge nourishes the intelligence, and even if intelligence shows us the right path, we must be strong enough to implement its directions. It is always desirable that *buddhi* be accompanied by *bala* and *vidya*. Most of the limitations in human life can be overcome by the trio *bala-buddhi-vidya*. However, problems don't disappear completely; they keep recurring. Only divine grace can root them out completely, and hence a prayer to remove pain and deformities – *klesha and vikara*.

All these explanations seem reasonable from a real-life perspective. As we have discussed, Tulsidas has set his objective in the very first verse itself. He wants self-realization, and that is his one-point agenda. It is a long, arduous journey, and he has placed a list of things that any average human being would need on the way. At the top of the list is intelligence; an intelligence that propels our entire being towards the consciousness or soul. The senses play havoc with the process by constantly pulling us downwards, and they listen only to spiritual strength that can restrain them. The path is full of confusion and illusions. Only knowledge that can distinguish what is truly good from what appears to be pleasant can help us reach our destination. This is the spiritual significance of seeking *bala-buddhi-vidya* from Hanuman ji.

The concept of *klesha* has its origin in the tradition of Yoga. *Klesha* is loosely translated as pain or affliction. Patanjali in his *Yogasutra* talks about five kinds of *klesha*: *avidya* or ignorance, *asmita* or ego, *raga* or attachment, *dvesha* or aversion and *abhinivesha* or clinging to life. Ignorance is the key member among all the *kleshas, giving* rise to the other four. Taken together, they are thought to be impediments to *yoga sadhana*. Maharshi Patanjali has suggested kriya yoga as a remedy to get rid of the *kleshas*. Kriya yoga is based on *tapa*, *svadhyaya,* and *Ishvara pranidhana*. So, when Tulsidas is praying to Sri Hanuman to remove his *klesha*, he, in reality, is asking the boons of austerity, self-study and surrender to God.

Vikara literally means any modification or mutation of our true self. In fact, the entire creation is a *vikara* of the Supreme Soul. Leading traditions of *Sanatan Darshana,* such as *Samkhya, Yoga, Advaita,* and even other systems like *Ayurveda* and *Shiksha,* speak of *vikaras*. The most popular philosophy is that of the Vedanta school, which lists six *vikaras* such as existence, birth, growth, modification, decay and death. But if we continue with the sense of the current verse, *vikara* for Goswami ji is probably disturbances in the equilibrium of the body and mind in the form of diseases or mental agitation.

In short, the couple of introductory *dohas* set the objective of the next forty verses, and they have a very strong flavour of knowledge-based philosophy mixed with the sweetness of unconditional devotion.

ॐ

SECTION II

Verses 1 to 10

1. जय हनुमान ज्ञान गुन सागर।
जय कपीस तिहुँ लोक उजागर ॥

Victory to Hanuman ji, the ocean of knowledge and virtues. Victory to the king of Vanaras, who is famous in the three worlds.

Immediately after the introductory *dohas* end, the *chaupais* begin with a poetic illustration of Hanuman as an ocean of knowledge and virtues. Being a storehouse of both learning and nobility is a rare achievement. It speaks about His *vinaya bhava.* In spite of being an ocean of knowledge, He does not have qualities like arrogance or anger. The very first mention of Hanuman ji in the *Chalisa* has been in the context of *buddhi* – the poet recalls Maruti as he thinks himself to be lacking in intelligence. And here, the very first image of the Lord is a Divinity full of *jnana*. Tulsidas, the master of integration, has carefully crafted the imagery of *Jnani Hanuman* juxtaposed against that of the very famous *Bhakta* and *Veera Hanuman*.

Ramayana is full of episodes that place Hanuman ji as the foremost among the learned ones. In the Valmiki Ramayana, the event that best justifies the ***Jnani Hanuman*** is an episode in the *Kishkindha Kanda* - the first meeting between Him and the brothers Sri Rama and Lakshmana. After listening to Hanuman for the first time, Rama makes an analysis of His character and tells

Lakshmana, “One who is not well versed in the *Rig, Yajur* and *Sama Vedas* and one who has not learnt grammar in its entirety, can never speak like this. Not a single word spoken by Him seems to be out of place. He speaks so well that even an enemy with a raised sword will start loving Him.”

Even Goswami ji is full of praise for such a knowledgeable God. He calls Maruti a *Vedantavid*, *Veda-Vedangavid* and *Brahmavadi* in the *Vinay Patrika*. In another hymn in the same text, He extols the Lord as a singer of the Sama Veda and an expert in *Nigama, Agama, Vyakarana, Kavya Kautuka,* and so on. The expertise of Hanuman ji extends even to the fields of drama, poetry and vocal music, as attested by the other compositions of Tulsidas and the *Narada Purana*.

But how could a Vanara earn such degrees? When and where did Anjaneya have His schooling? The *Hanuman Bahuk*, another masterpiece of forty-four verses by Tulsidas, briefly narrates how Anjaneya learnt all the *vidyas*. As per the legend, He went to Surya Deva and requested Him to be His preceptor. However, the ever-busy Sun God did not take Him seriously. Surya Deva was required to travel constantly, so how could a disciple face Him and receive the schooling? The young Maruti had a solution – He started walking backwards while facing the moving Sun and completed His learning without committing any error.

And we must not forget that Hanuman ji was the only person on site, other than Arjuna, when the Bhagavat Gita was being revealed. Though the event belonged to a later yuga, the supreme knowledge imparted by Lord Krishna must have enriched the immortal Anjaneya.

The word "Ujagara" is used across Indian languages with two broad meanings. *Ujagara* in Hindi mostly means something that shines brightly or something brilliant. It is also used for someone who is renowned or famous. In many regional languages like Odia and Marathi, the term is used to convey a meaning of wakefulness or a sense of protective vigilance. While *Jagara* in Sanskrit means wakeful or vigilant, a slightly different word, "Ujjagara", means one who is excited. The *Mahaviri Vyakhya* goes with the meaning *prasiddha* or famous for this word. Even Goswami ji has used the term as a synonym for "famous" in the *Ramcharitmanas*. (*Bandhaa setu Nala Nila naagara, Rama kripa jasu bhayau ujaagara*)

The verse is a salutation to the God who is famous in the three worlds because of His humility and the brilliance of His knowledge.

2. राम दूत अतुलित बल धामा।
अंजनि पुत्र पवनसुत नामा॥

O messenger of Rama, Son of Anjana and Son of Pavana Deva, You are an abode of incomparable strength.

Sri Hanuman has been a *duta* or messenger twice in the Ramayana. He became Sugreeva's messenger and went to meet the brothers Rama and Lakshmana. The interaction was not only life-changing for Hanuman, but it also decided the course of all the future events in the epic. And even more famous than this is His role as the emissary of Rama to Lanka. In the Ramayana, an entire *kanda* or canto is dedicated to Maruti's flight to Lanka and His amazing deeds on the island. And out of all the cantos, the one dedicated to the *Rama Duta,* i.e., the *Sundara Kanda,* is the only one to be recited as a stand- alone chapter by devotees even today.

Here, Tulsidas adds one more attribute, a storehouse of unparalleled strength, to someone who is already an ocean of knowledge and virtues. As discussed in the beginning, the first ten verses build an image on which the devotee is supposed to meditate on his *Ishta Deva.* And in the process of image-building, knowledge comes before strength.

3. महाबीर बिक्रम बजरंगी।
कुमति निवार सुमति के संगी॥

O great hero with powerful strides and a vajra-hard body, You are a dispeller of evil thoughts and a companion of good ones.

Mahavira is an expression commonly used for anyone with heroic deeds and great power. Many of the warriors in our *Itihasa* and *Purana* have been addressed with this epithet. Legends of Hanuman are full of heroic deeds, particularly in the face of extreme challenges. These accounts have become so popular that today, the term is used almost exclusively for Him. The word *Vira* also has a tantric connotation – addressing Maruti as *Mahavira* points towards His worship in the Tantric tradition.

The word *Vikrama* has its origin in the Sanskrit root "Kram". Though loosely translated as valour or strength, it is part of a very ancient Rig Vedic concept meaning *to step forward*, *stride through* or *to advance*. Vedic Vishnu is associated with this idea, and the later *Puranic* story of the *Vamana Avatara* putting His foot forward to cover all the three worlds is an echo of this concept. In the context of Hanuman, it points towards His unmatched strength. *Vikrama* should also mean His very famous aerial strides: to the Sun God from the Earth, to Lanka from the Indian mainland, and to the Himalayas from Lanka.

Bajrang Bali or Bajrangi is a very popular name of Hanuman in North India. Literally, it means "the one with a body as hard as the vajra". In the Sanatan tradition, Indra is the owner of a very strong weapon called the *Vajra* or the thunderbolt, and anything strong is usually mentioned as *vajra-hard*. As per the Valmiki Ramayana, Hanuman, as a kid, had successfully survived the strike of the *vajra*. So, it is natural that His body would be at least equal to the *vajra* in hardness.

The term *Mati* conveys a meaning of thought, intention or the mind. Here, Anjaneya is being invoked as the one who destroys evil thoughts and brings in good and pious ones. In the path of bhakti, the intention of the devotee is the only thing that matters, and to keep the intention pure, Goswami ji resorts to the Son of the Wind God. Continuing with His dominance over the mind-space, Anjaneya is also believed to cure diseases of the mind or psychiatric disorders. For ages, He has been the go-to deity for all kinds of mental disturbances and illnesses.

This is a strange verse in the sense that it conjoins two different aspects of Maruti. While the first half describes Him as an extremely powerful deity, with specific reference to His physical strength, the second half is a prayer urging Him to bring in purity of thoughts. His blessing works wonders on both the physical and mental planes.

4. कंचन बरन बिराज सुबेसा।
कानन कुंडल कुँचित केसा॥

You have a golden-hued body and a pleasing appearance, with earrings and curly hair.

Using the expression *kanchana varana* for someone is a way to describe an unblemished and radiating skin tone, a golden complexion. This metaphor has been commonly used in ancient Indian literature since the Vedic age. While Mahadeva is *Karpura Gaura* or fair as camphor, Radha Rani is *Tapta Kanchana Gaurangi* or fair with a complexion of molten gold. Hanuman ji was born to a very good-looking mother; she used to be an

Apsara in her previous life. Moreover, being the son of a Deva, Hanuman is naturally handsome.

In the *Sundara Kanda* of Valmiki Ramayana, we get some more details about the appearance of Anjaneya. Though medieval literature associates red-coloured robes with Him, Valmiki's Hanuman was wearing a white dress and was shining like a bundle of thunderbolts during His expedition to Lanka. His eyes were golden coloured. Valmiki describes Him as having both a yellowish and a reddish complexion. In fact, His golden complexion helped Him to hide within a similarly coloured *Simshapa* tree in the *Ashoka Vanika*.

Even the Mahabharata has some details on His appearance. There is a very famous story about Bhima meeting Hanuman while wandering in the Himalayas. On Bhima's request, Hanuman displayed His gigantic form, and Bhima could hardly bear the sight of His extremely bright yellowish-brown appearance. He was shining like a bundle of lightning. *Kanchana varana* probably relates more to His effulgence rather than the complexion proper.

Some of the regional versions of the Ramayana tell us that Anjaneya was born with *upavita, kundala* and *kaupina*. Even though the Valmiki Ramayana has no details of a pair of earrings as part of His adornments, the Kamban Ramayana does speak about it. In the second chapter of the *Kishkindha Kandam*, we find the description of a kundala-wearing Hanuman. He was in the guise of a *vipra* during His first meeting with the Raghu brothers in Kishkindha. When Anjaneya returned to His original form, He grew so high that the Brothers could not see His face or His glittering earrings.

If we go by the descriptions of the Telugu *Ranganatha Ramayana*, Anjaneya does wear a pair of beautiful earrings. As per the text, when Hanuman approached the brothers in the guise of a *vatu*, Sri Rama exclaimed about His beautiful appearance (*suvesha*) with golden complexion (*kanchana varana*), earrings (*kundala*), sacred thread (*janeu*), bracelet, necklace, and so on. Later on, when both the parties got to know each other, Hanuman revealed the words of Lord Brahma. The Grandfather had prophesied, "Know Him to be Your master who would be able to see Your adornments". This suggests that Anjaneya's *kundala* was a *divya abhushana* or a divine ornament, and it always remained beyond the sight of mortals.

Lutgendorf argues that *kundala* links Hanuman to the *Natha Yogi* tradition. Natha yogis were part of the *Shaiva* tradition but had a great influence on the *Ramanandi* sect of Vaishnavas. A kundala-wearing Hanuman is thus a solid bridge between the Vaishnava and Shaiva *parampara*.

Yaksha idols are often seen with large earrings. Some Indologists believe that Yakshas were worshipped by the indigenous population of northern India and were integrated into the mainstream culture in the subsequent centuries. A mace-holding guardian deity with prominent earrings, placed at temple entrances and along the peripheries of villages and cities, fits into the image of both Maruti and a Yaksha. All these nuances in the short text of the Hanuman Chalisa prove the poet's eagerness to weave the contrasting threads of Indian culture into a single fabric.

The *Mahaviri Vyakhya* argues that this cannot be the description of Sri Hanuman in His natural form. It relates to His *Brahmana* guise, which He had to take during His first meeting with Rama-Lakshmana, as well as with Vibhishana.

The *Chalisa* is probably the only text that speaks about Anjaneya's curly hair. Not much scriptural reference exists on this aspect of the Lord. In a very rare iconographic representation, the idol of the famous Balaji at Salasar in Rajasthan shows Him with a moustache and beard.

When we sit down and close our eyes to pray, this verse gives us some idea of the appearance of our beloved Hanuman ji.

5. हाथ बज्र औ ध्वजा बिराजै।
कांधे मूँज जनेउ साजै॥

You hold a mace and a banner in your hands. You wear a sacred thread made of munja on your shoulder.

Moving further ahead with physical appearance, three more adornments of Anjaneya are added in this verse – a mace or *gada*, a flag and a sacred thread.

Lord Indra is often depicted as the holder of the ***Vajra***, which has been interpreted both as an indestructible weapon and the thunderbolt. The *gada* that we know today is undoubtedly different from Lord Indra's weapon. But almost all the major languages across the Indo-European family refer to a club or a mace when the term *Vajra* is used. Surprisingly, the Valmiki Ramayana has not portrayed Hanuman with a mace, even though the later age iconography has made the weapon an inseparable part of Him. Valmiki's Hanuman fought all major battles with His bare hands or, at best, with large rocks, uprooted trees and pillars as His weapon. Goswami ji himself has addressed Him as "*Bhujabala*" while narrating episodes of His fight with the demons in Lanka. The *Vanaras* probably did not use such weapons, and that's why there is no mention of a mace, even in the famous duel between Vali and Sugreeva.

Even archaeological findings in the subcontinent have corroborated that the concept of mace-holding Hanuman is a relatively modern one. Today, we find His idols with a mace in the left or right hand, mace raised above the head, one placed gently on the thigh or the tip held firmly to the ground, and so on. However, none of the ancient idols from the first millennium CE show Him holding the weapon.

Another deity who is depicted as holding a mace is Kuvera. He is the king of Yakshas and is very closely related to Lord Shiva. A *mudgara* may not be exactly the same as a mace, but it resembles a mace very closely. A *gada* or *mudgara* is an integral part of Yaksha iconography. Very ancient idols of Yakshas have often been named *Mudgarapani,* or the one holding a mace. The idea of mace-holding Hanuman was introduced in the medieval age to validate His yaksha origin and also as an effort to bring in Vaishnava–Shaiva integration.

If we ignore the accounts of the *Uttara Ramayana*, Hanuman ji has not participated in any direct combat after the Lanka war. Even in the Mahabharata war, His role was limited to terrifying the enemies by producing a loud sound and absorbing the negativities of all the weapons fired at Arjuna's chariot. In the *Kali Yuga*, He has probably assumed the responsibility of restoring order in this chaotic world. The *vajra* that Goswamiji's Hanuman holds is a symbol of His immense physical strength, His absolute control over the senses, and His stewardship over the planet in which we live.

A *Dhvaja* is a flag or a banner. It can be fixed on a chariot or can be held in hand. The royal flag of Ayodhya had the symbol of the *Kovidara* tree, which is almost identical to today's *Kachnar* or the mountain ebony tree. But Rama did not have the royal army during His fight in Lanka, nor did He have any chariots. Even Sugreeva did not have chariots during the war. All they had were millions of *Vanaras* who walked barefoot. Even during their march on the *Nala Setu* towards Lanka, there is no mention of the *Vanaras* holding a banner in the Valmiki Ramayana. The *Ramopakhyana,* a brief retelling of the Ramayana within the Mahabharata, does, however, speak of the marching *Vanara Sena* as "Vahula Dhvajam", and most likely, this phrase is the origin of the banner-holding Maruti of Tulsidas.

Goswami ji has used the epithet *Bhanu-Kulabhanu-Kirati Pataka* for Anjaneya in his writings. *Dhvaja* should be taken as a metaphor for Rama's invincibility on the battlefield and His unblemished glory. And who could have been a better flag bearer of Sri Rama's strength and glory than The Son of the Wind God!

Munja is a type of grass belonging to the wild sugarcane family named variously as *Sarkanda, Kash* or *Kashatandi* in Indian languages. It was specifically used to make *upavita,* or the sacred thread, in ancient times. Though other plants like the *Murva* or the Indian Bowstring hemp were also used, *Munja* was so common and popular that it almost became a synonym for the sacred thread. *Munja Janeu* should mean a *janeu* made from the fibres of wild sugarcane, *Saccharum bengalense.*

The *Anushashana parva* of the Mahabharata tells us that a *vipra* should wear a sacred thread made from *Munja* fibres, a warrior should use *Murva,* and a trader should wear the same made from *Valvaja* or hemp. *Munja Janeu* symbolizes the "Vipratva" of Sri Hanuman. He is an *akhanda brahmachari*, but more importantly, He is a bestower of *Atma Jnana*. Tulsidas, the master of integration, never fails to integrate the *Jnani* Hanuman with His more popular *Veera* and *Bhakta* persona. The Hanuman of the *Chalisa* is a fighter who ensures peace and order, a flag bearer of Sri Rama's ideas and policies, and one who has attained self-realization through knowledge and control of senses. The combination of *vajra, dhvaja* and *janeu* represents this extraordinary personality.

**6. शंकर सुवन केसरी नंदन।
तेज प्रताप महा जगवंदन॥**

You are an incarnation of Mahadeva, O Son of Keshari. The whole world reveres Your great strength and valour.

This is another verse related to the curriculum vitae of Hanuman ji. This verse has been a matter of debate for two reasons. Did Tulsidas use the word *Suvana,* or was it something else in the original version? This is the first issue. Secondly, how do we make sense of the parentage of Hanuman ji, given the fact that He is related to so many Divinities?

Scholarly opinions vary on the use of the word "Suvana" here. *Suuvan* (सूवन्) in Sanskrit is an adjective with a connotation of childbearing or generating, while *Suvana* (सुवन) has three meanings – the Sun, the Moon and fire. The *Mahaviri Vyakhya* favours "swayam" over *suvana*. Tulsidas has used the term सुवन and not सूवन्, probably in the interest of metrical rules in a regional language. And that he very much means to convey the idea of "the Son of Sri Shankara" or "an Avatara of Sri Shankara" is evident from his composition, the *Vinay Patrika*. In literary circles, the stature of the *Vinay Patrika* is considered second only to the *Ramcharitmanas* among Goswamiji's compositions. It begins with *Ganesha Stuti,* and the very first line in this prayer has the term *Shankara Suvana* addressed to Lord Ganapati (गाइये गनपति जगबंदन । संकर-सुवन भवानी नंदन). And the very same *Vinay Patrika* addresses Hanuman both as *Keshari Suvana* and *Rudra Avatara*.

In the second verse of the *Chalisa*, Hanuman is already addressed as *Anjani Putra* and *Pavana Suta. Putra*, *Suta*, and *Nandana* are all considered synonyms, even though the sense they carry differs from each other. *Putra* is one who, by performing all the prescribed rituals for the departed soul, saves his parents from a particular station in hell known as *Put.* So, he should be seen as a protector in the afterlife. *Suta* is someone who has taken birth or who came forth from his parents; he is a part of the parents' body. *Suvana* should carry the same meaning as *suta*. And the synonym *Nandana* is used to describe someone who brings joy to our life, of course, the present life. The fountainhead of divine thoughts that inspired Goswami ji to choose his words does not belong to this world. We can never earn the qualification to peek into that. But at least we can say that he has chosen the synonyms for the word "son" based on the beat or *matra* of Indian poetry.

Now, let us examine the second issue – how should we look at Hanumanji's origin? Philip Lutgendorf believes that Maruti is a second-generation deity, an offspring of another God, just like Ganesha and Kartikeya.

Therefore, His birth stories figure very prominently in mythology. And a plethora of birth stories exist about Him because they add to His curriculum vitae.

As per the Valmiki Ramayana, Anjana was an Apsara named *Punjikasthala*, who was born as a *Vanara*. She was the daughter of Kunjara and was married to a leader of the *Vanaras* named Keshari. Once, she was roaming alone on a mountain top, and Vayu Devata got attracted towards her. He embraced her through the mind – मनसा अस्मि गतो यत् त्वाम् परिष्वज्य यशस्विनि - and she gave birth to Hanuman ji. We do not have too many details, but the text of the Valmiki Ramayana suggests that Hanuman was born almost immediately after the event. So, it was a divine conception that happened at the level of the mind and not a regular human or even a *Vanara* birth. Valmiki does not give any direct reference to Hanuman being *Rudra Avatara*.

The *Shata Rudra Samhita* of the *Shiva Purana* is an ancient text. It is probably the first Indian scripture that relates Anjaneya as an *amsha* of Mahadeva. Lord Shiva was desirous of helping Sri Rama in His human incarnation. Once, He saw Lord Vishnu in the *Mohini* form and became captivated by the cosmic beauty. Vayu Deva was entrusted with the task of implanting the seeds of life that came from Mahadeva. Anjana was the daughter of the sage Gautama. The Wind God placed Lord Shiva's life seeds in Anjana's ears, and she gave birth to Hanuman later on. Again, the birth is not at all natural here. But what the *Shiva Purana* tries to tell us is that Hanuman ji owes His origin to both Shiva and Vishnu.

Skanda Purana, the biggest among the *Mahapuranas*, says that it was Nandi who was born as Hanuman during the Ramayana era.

Ananda Ramayana has a very strange description of the legend. A divine *payasam* was prepared for Dasharatha's *putreshti yajna*. Only the three queens of Ayodhya were supposed to drink it. However, Vayu Devata took a portion of it and dropped it over Anjana's hands. And thereafter, Anjana gave birth to Hanuman.

Tracing Hanuman's origin to both the Lords Shiva and Vishnu takes us to another ancient character in the Sanatan tradition. Vrishakapi is a part-human, part-animal (mostly monkey) character present since the time of the Rig Veda. Though he was initially styled as a friend or son of Lord Indra, the later scriptures linked him with both Shiva and Vishnu. As per the *Brahma Purana*, Indra was defeated and imprisoned by Mahashani, the son of Daitya Hiranya. At Varuna's request, Mahashani released Indra but inflicted a lot of humiliation on Him. Indrani suggested that Indra go to the confluence of the Phena and Godavari rivers and pray to Sri Vishnu and Mahadeva. Vrishakapi, a product of the combined blessings of the two Gods, arose from the water and killed Mahashani.

Over the course of time, the legend of Vrishakapi became so famous that the title was used as a synonym for any God who was considered very powerful. How Hanuman ji came to the pantheon of Indian Gods and

Goddesses will always remain a matter of debate, but Vrishakapi is surely a forerunner of the concept of Hanuman.

Whatever may be the fact behind His origin, Maruti draws His identity from two *Vanaras* – Anjana and Keshari, and His unmatched strength from three Devas – Vayu, Vishnu and Shiva.

Just as in the second verse, where His unparalleled power (atulita bal dhama) is stitched with Anjana and *Pavana Deva*, here, in the sixth verse, His great strength and valour have been linked with Lord Shiva and Keshari. Destiny probably needed an entity who could withstand even the strongest of negative forces like Ravana and Kumbhakarna, one who could outperform all the agents of darkness in strength and wit, and one who could perform deeds unthinkable even for the Gods. In addition, He was destined to be a Chiranjeevi, and this means the storehouse of strength had to be imperishable. In the background of such a grand divine plan, Hanuman ji had to draw His strength from multiple and the best of the best sources – hence the legend of multiple birth stories.

7. बिद्यावान गुनी अति चातुर।
राम काज करिबे को आतुर॥

You are knowledgeable, virtuous and very clever. You always stay excited to carry out Rama's tasks.

This is the seventh verse, and we have already seen Hanuman as a repository of knowledge and virtues. The poet just goes on adding more to the image. Another attribute that is mentioned here is *chaturai* – smartness or cleverness. In the context of Anjaneya, it is related more to the application of knowledge during hours of crisis. Knowing very well that "Ati Chatura" could be misinterpreted as cunning or shrewd, Tulsidas has placed *Vidyavan* and *Guni* before it. Goswami ji aims to create an aura of smartness combined with humility and a sense of responsibility.

The stories of Hanuman's smartness are many. The display of an outstanding communication skill during the first meeting with the Raghava brothers, engaging with deities and demons with equal ease while crossing the ocean, voluntary submission to the *Brahmastra* so that He could have a chance to persuade Ravana for Sita's release – all these bear a stamp of His legendary smartness. In fact, all the recorded conversations of Maruti in the Ramayana are epitomes of cleverness.

Perhaps the best among them is His advice to Ravana in the court of Lanka. There is not an iota of fear or confusion when He talks to Ravana, the fiercest of the demons, in his own court. Hanuman initiates the conversation by addressing Ravana as *Prabhu* and says, "I have come here as a messenger of *your brother* Sugreeva". Even an enemy will feel elated after listening to these respectful words! Then He slowly starts exerting pressure on the demon king, "You must be knowing Vali, the king of *Vanaras*. This is for your information that he has been killed by Sri Rama". Just imagine the mindset of Ravana when he hears that Vali, who was even his tormentor, has been killed by Rama! Like a seasoned diplomat, Anjaneya changes the tone and becomes respectful again. He addresses Ravana as *Mahaprajna,* or the greatly intelligent one, and continues, "You have earned this unmatched prosperity through great *tapasya*. Why are you hellbent on destroying all these? Abducting someone else's wife does not at all suit an intelligent person like you." Hanuman continues to make him understand the strength of Sri Rama by talking about the killing of Khara-Dushana and Vali and also the friendship between Sugreeva and the Raghu prince. After building the pressure gradually with intermittent words of appreciation, He finishes the talk with a direct warning – "Do not think of Sita as a helpless lady who is staying under your captivity. Know Her as *Kala Ratri,* who will destroy your entire kingdom."

Today, even the greatest of diplomats would take this conversation as inspiring.

He starts with being respectful so that an impressed Ravana would agree to engage in conversation with a *Vanara* and not discard Him outright. He follows it with an indirect threat by taking Vali's name, only to rekindle some unpleasant memories. Here, Maruti's intention is to arouse a little fear. A frightened Ravana would continue to listen, to ensure that there is no bad news anymore. Hanuman changes the tone once more and becomes respectful again. Ravana is the personification of ego. Only adjectives like *Mahaprajna* can keep him on the discussion table, even though he is being made to listen to the greatness of his enemy. Availing this window of opportunity, Maruti counsels Ravana about the futility of his conflict with Rama. Then, He goes on to enumerate Rama's strengths, and concludes the session with a direct threat. His last words equating Sita with *Devi Kalaratri* are obviously meant to warn Ravana of dire consequences.

What a way to make one's enemy listen to a messenger!

When the poet of the Hanuman Chalisa says that Hanuman always stays excited to perform any of the tasks related to Sri Rama, he actually means "more than excited, to the point of being restless." That is what the term *Atura* conveys. And another interesting thing about Hanuman ji is that whenever He is entrusted to carry out something for His *Prabhu*, He does a little more than what is required. He was supposed to go to Lanka and come back, just with the information on Sita's whereabouts; at least, that was what Sugreeva had instructed Pavana Kumara. But see how this devotee of Raghuvara executed the task assigned to Him! He destroyed a few buildings and gardens, killed a portion of the enemy army and even killed a son of the enemy king, issued a direct threat to the abductor, did a first-rate espionage about the strength and weakness of Lanka, identified potential allies in the form of Vibhishana and finally came back to the base camp in mainland India.

When asked to bring a few lifesaving herbs, Hanuman returned carrying the entire mountain peak. Of course, every minute was precious, and the deities presiding over the Himalayan plants did not cooperate at the first contact. But we must accept that only someone who is *Atura* to perform His Prabhu's task can work such wonders!

8. प्रभु चरित्र सुनिबे को रसिया।
राम लखन सीता मनबसिया॥

You enjoy listening to the life story of Your Master.
Rama, Lakshmana and Sita dwell in Your heart.

The English interpretation of the word *Rasiya* is someone who likes to enjoy pleasures and is a lover of good things in life. As long as Sri Rama was there in this world, Hanuman's day job was to guard Him, and to assist Him in all possible ways. And His favourite pastime was listening to the glory of Raghava. The story goes that when *Rama Avatara* neared its end, Maruti was given the option to accompany Rama to His sacred abode. But He refused the offer and opted to stay back on this planet instead. His logic was – "Let me have the pleasure of listening to *Rama Nama* as long as it continues in the world. I am not very sure if I can have that in Your *Parama Dhama*. For me, listening to Your name is more pleasurable than living in Your proximity".

The second line of the verse can be interpreted in two different ways. Rama, Lakshmana and Sita reside within Hanuman's heart, and He stays within Their hearts.

Either way, it implies the extreme devotion that Hanuman had for them. A very famous story tells us that Hanuman ji tore apart His heart to show the image of Sita-Rama. The legend owes its origin to the fifteenth-century Bengali text *Krittivasa Ramayana*, composed by the celebrated Bengali poet Krittivasa Ojha. The text mentions the episode just before the end of *Lanka Kanda.*

After the coronation of Rama in Ayodhya, all the *Vanaras* were awarded with gifts of all kinds. Only Hanuman was sitting silently, with His eyes closed. As expected, He was a bit sad as He did not receive any gift. And then Sita took out Her priceless necklace and gave it to Him. She blessed Hanuman with immortality and also blessed that He would be present at every session of *Rama Katha*.

After getting the necklace, Hanuman started tearing it and chewing the jewels. An annoyed Lakshmana complained to Sri Rama about this and wanted to know why such a precious gift was bestowed upon a *Vanara* who did not understand its value. A smiling Rama redirected the question to Hanuman. Hanuman answered that He was throwing them away as He did not find the name of His *Prabhu* in any of the jewels. Getting further irritated with this answer, Lakshmana asked, "But Your body does not have the name of Rama, then why are You still alive?". Hanuman, the epitome of bhakti, responded by tearing apart His chest with His nails. The whole assembly saw the bones of His chest inscribed with millions and millions of *Rama-Nama*.

In the subsequent centuries, the legend was translated into Hanuman iconography with a modification - *Rama Nama* got replaced with the image of Sita-Rama. The popularity of this episode has continued well into the present time, and one can spot the *images of Sita Rama inside Hanuman's chest* printed on book covers, wall calendars, key chains, and so on.

9. सूक्ष्म रूप धरि सियहि दिखावा।
विकट रूप धरि लंक जरावा॥

You appeared in a minute form before Sita and assumed a formidable shape while setting Lanka on fire.

10. भीम रूप धरि असुर सँहारे।
रामचंद्र के काज सँवारे॥

You assumed a terrible form while killing the demons. You accomplish all of Rama's tasks.

The ninth and the tenth verses talk about three forms of the Lord. A very minute (*sukshma*) form, which He assumed while meeting Sita in the *Ashoka Vanika*; a formidable (*vikata*) appearance while setting fire to the city of Lanka and a terrible (*bhima*) form while killing the demons. Apart from the context in which these forms were displayed, these lines point towards the *siddhi* attained by Hanumanji. He is capable of changing His form as per wish and as per the need of the circumstance. In Yogic parlance, these accomplishments are known as *anima*, *mahima*, *laghima* and *garima*, representing the ability to make oneself very small, very large, very light, and very heavy, respectively.

When Hanuman entered Lanka to look for Sita, He had assumed a very small form; all the versions of the Ramayana agree on this. But the texts differ from each other on exactly how small he had become.

There is some confusion here with regard to Valmiki's account of the *Sukshma rupa*. The critical edition of the text uses the term *Prisadamshaka* (one which stings an antelope), whereas other available manuscripts call it *Vrishadamshaka (one which bites or stings a bull)*. Bibek Debroy, in his English translation of the Critical Edition of the Valmiki Ramayana, has suggested three different meanings of these words: a gnat or a similar insect, a cat, and a dog. The *Ramcharitmanas* describes Him to be equal to a *mashaka* or a mosquito in size. Another popular text, the *Adhyatma Ramayana*, compares the size of Hanuman to that of a *Kalavinka* or sparrow. Out of all these, the cat-sized Hanuman is the most popular one in folklore. If we analyse the chronology of the scriptures, there is a gradual reduction of Hanuman's size from that of a cat through a sparrow and finally to the size of a mosquito. Catherine Ludvik has put it as follows: "Anjaneya is gradually being given greater power, for the smaller the form, the more places it can enter and the lesser the likelihood of its being noticed."

A very interesting observation in the *Valmiki Ramayana* is that of a commotion created in the *Ashoka Garden* when Hanuman entered it to look for Sita. Even if He was the size of a small cat or an insect, the trees could not bear His weight and started shedding flowers and leaves; it created a false sense of springtime in the garden. How does one make sense of Valmiki's narration? Well, Hanuman had used *anima siddhi* to reduce His body size, but probably had not resorted to *laghima* to make Himself light. And there was absolutely no reduction in His physical power. Otherwise, Lanka Devi would not have fallen down unconscious with a mere fist attack by a mosquito or even a cat-sized *Vanara*!

And Sita was naturally suspicious of noticing a miniature *Vanara* talking in chaste Sanskrit, narrating the glory of Her husband. Moreover, She did not feel very optimistic when Hanuman assured that Raghava would rescue Her with the help of *Vanaras*. The Son of the Wind God had to demonstrate His *Virat Rupa* to gain Sita's confidence. Tulsidas describes this *Virat rupa* as an extremely powerful and terrible one, resembling a huge golden mountain - कनक-भूधराकार शरीरा। समर-भयंकर अतिबल बीरा. So, in reality, Hanuman had displayed both His minute and gigantic forms to Vaidehi.

Now, let us consider Maruti's *Vikata rupa,* which He assumed while setting the city of Lanka on fire. There are at least two episodes of *Lanka Dahana* in the Valmiki Ramayana. The first one is the more famous; it happened during Hanuman's solo journey to the island.

The second attack happened on the very night when Lakshmana was revived by the *Sanjivanee* herb. It was actually Sugreeva's brain-child, and a group of *Vanaras* participated in it along with Hanuman. In all likelihood, it inflicted more damage to the city than the first one, but our focus in this book is on the first episode.

When fire was set to His tail, Hanuman was tied with ropes made of hemp and tree bark. As soon as it happened, He attained a gigantic form, and then swiftly reduced His body size to get rid of the ropes. Again, He went back to His gigantic form and started jumping from building to building, setting the entire city on fire. The flames emanating from the blazing tail mimicked a garland of fire, and He was shining like the radiant Sun. It might be a good poetic description of His *vikata rupa,* but the horror that would have pervaded the minds of the demon population during that time can never be captured in words.

Goswami ji does not come up with this much detail in the *Ramcharitmanas,* but he does make another interesting observation. During *Lanka Dahana*, Hanuman ji had resorted to both *mahima* and *laghima* siddhis. His body had enlarged to gigantic proportions, but had also become very light, both at the same time - देह बिसाल परम हरुआई. And no doubt, it would have given Him a significant advantage while leaping from building to building. This is the *application of siddhi* at its best and clearly justifies His name, *Siddha Mahavira.*

The *Hanuman Bahuk*, another timeless composition by the great saint-poet, begins with the idea of the *Vikata rupa*. Hanuman is addressed as the God with a terrible face and teeth, yellow eyes, and a coarse tail. Tulsidas invokes this dreadful form in the hope that it will dispel sufferings and pain. Maruti is not only an ardent follower of His master's orders but also a fierce protector of His devotees against everything evil. The *vikata rupa* serves both purposes.

The third form is the terrible or the *bhima rupa,* which He assumed while fighting the demons. Anjaneya had killed many of them during the Rama-Ravana war, but this description probably refers to His solo performance in the *Sundara Kanda*. After accomplishing the assigned task of meeting Sita, Hanuman ji displayed His terrible form, which was both gigantic and fierce, at the same time. He went on uprooting trees, crushing the hilltops and destroying buildings. He leapt over an arched doorway, pulled up a huge iron bar from the arch and started killing the demons with that. Taking the strike further, He ascended a huge building and increased His body size to an even higher level. He had become so huge that the demons were falling down on the ground with the mere clapping of His hands. Tales of His *bhima rupa* in the *Sundara Kanda* are full of descriptions of how He killed the demons: striking them with His bare hands, crushing them on His thighs, and hitting them with huge rocks, trees, uprooted iron bars and pillars. He utilised almost everything large available by His side as a weapon. For most of this episode, He stayed on top of the arched doorway near the garden. This is just a glimpse of Maruti's *bhima rupa*.

When we think of His *sukshma*, *vikata* and *bhima rupas*, it is natural that the associated physical aspects come to our mind. But even more important than these physical forms are the thoughts that drove Him to assume these *rupas*. The poetic description of the reasoning algorithms that played inside Anjaneya's mind before assuming each of these forms is one of the best in world literature.

During the flight over the ocean, Maruti was in His gigantic form. Just before landing, He thought – "Looking at my huge size and great speed, the demons might get curious. Let me go back to my usual form". Therefore, He was in His usual form at the time of landing on the *Lamba* Mountain in Lanka.

He took some time to have an overview of the city, and the algorithm continued: "This city seems to be very well protected by cruel and powerful demons. The security here is so tight that even air cannot enter without their permission. Is there a way to find the Princess without being spotted by Ravana? The guards are *mayavi* demons themselves; any attempt to trick them by taking the disguise of a demon will not work here.

I have to outsmart these terrible guards while searching for Sita. And once I find Her, I have to wait for a one-to-one meeting with the Princess in a place devoid of demons. But, getting harmed is sure if I continue to stay here in my usual form. And if I am harmed, the objective of my master will also get shattered.

At this moment, I am a messenger, and the success of the mission depends on my decision-making. I should not think too much about profit and loss, nor should I fall into depression. I must wait for the opportune time and enter the city at night in a form that should be hardly noticeable for the rakshasas."

He waited patiently until late at night and then assumed a tiny form, like that of a cat.

Even more amazing is His reasoning before He assumed the *bhima rupa* to kill the demons. After He accomplished the task of meeting Sita, The Son of Vayu thought somewhat in this line: "I have almost completed my mission. But still, a little more remains to be achieved. Demons are my enemy here; they do not understand the language of negotiation (*Sama*). Here in Lanka, everybody is so rich that buying peace through gifts (*dana*) is just out of the question. And all of them are proud and strong warriors; I don't think I can sow the seeds of dissension (*bheda*) among them. They deserve to see my valour, and that is the only way left (*danda*).

Today, if I can somehow kill a few of their principal warriors, the Lankan army will get weakened in future wars. Moreover, it will give me an opportunity to see the ones who command the *rakshasa army*. But the end must not be unpleasant for me; my aim is to get Ravana's attention and respect. I want an audience with the demon king and to see how strong his army is. Let me start by destroying this beautiful garden, which is so dear to Ravana. Then he will send his soldiers, and a combat will ensue for sure."

What followed this algorithm is a very well-known story in itself. Hanuman assumed a gigantic form and started attacking the demons and destroying almost everything near the garden.

When fire was being set to His tail, what was going on inside Maruti's mind? He did not protest; instead, He made a quick mental calculation: "What else remains to be accomplished – something which can further increase the anguish of the demons? I have destroyed the garden, killed a portion of the army and even killed some of their excellent warriors. But the fort of Ravana, the very symbol of his authority, still remains untouched. If I succeed in destroying even a part of the fort, my Lord's job will become easy. They have put fire to my tail, and now it is my job to satisfy Agni Deva by bringing Him in contact with the excellent mansions of the city." Then, assuming the *bhima rupa*, He started jumping from building to building.

The term *kaaj savaare* is quite meaningful in the second line. Here, the connotation is something more than mere performance of a task. Doing something exceptional, making something right and beautiful that has gone wrong – these are the underlying meanings of the words.

Let us take just one of the tasks He was entrusted with. He was supposed to get information on Princess Sita, come back to India, and report to Sugreeva and Sri Rama. But His style of serving the master goes way beyond just accomplishing the task. In one go, and as a one-man army, He launched a multi-pronged attack on the strongest empire of that time.

See what *kaaj savaare* means to Sri Anjaneya!

On the ***Military*** front, He killed a sizeable portion of the rakshasa army and showed them that even their highest weapon, Brahmastra, could do no harm to Him. He burnt down their properties, destroyed a beautiful garden, and thereby inflicted a ***Financial*** burden on the kingdom. Aksha, the young son of the enemy king, was killed in the battle. It was a big ***Personal*** loss to Ravana. Hanuman sent a strong message to the king and the entire Lankan population about the strength of Rama's army. In a way, He defeated them mentally even before the actual Rama-Ravana war began. It was both a ***Political*** and a ***Diplomatic*** defeat for the island nation. In front of all his council of ministers, Ravana was lectured on the immorality of abducting someone else's wife. It denied the demon king a ***Moral*** high ground, if at all he had anything left of it.

The first ten verses play a very significant role in creating a visual narrative of Hanuman ji. We learn about His complexion, hairstyle, religious symbols, adornments, weapons, and other accessories that He carries. We also get an idea of His origin, and how and why He assumes different forms utilizing His yogic siddhis. And Goswami ji keeps suggesting that we think of Him as a God of knowledge, as much as a God of devotion and physical strength.

ॐ

SECTION III

Verses 11 to 20

As we discussed in the introduction, the poet wants to express a pattern of thought while organizing the content of the Hanuman Chalisa. Let's think of the *Chalisa* as a resume of Hanuman ji. The first quarter gives us His personal details, while the second quarter is about His special achievements, honours and testimonies from people who matter. From a deeper perspective, the introductory *dohas* lay out the objective of having Sri Hanuman along with the Raghava family in our hearts, and the first quarter builds an image of Him for us to contemplate upon. Now, the second quarter fixes our trust and devotion in Him by narrating His supreme achievements and accolades.

The second quarter of the *Chalisa* deals with five extraordinary deeds that Hanuman ji has performed. Three of them are about His aerial journey, which He made to accomplish some tasks or out of simple curiosity. The remaining two tell us how He was instrumental in bestowing kingship on two deserving persons.

11. लाय सजीवन लखन जियाये।
श्रीरघुबीर हरषि उर लाये॥

You brought the Sanjeevani herb and revived Lakshmana. The Hero of the Raghu Dynasty (Sri Rama) embraced You in joy.

12. रघुपति कीन्ही बहुत बड़ाई।
तुम मम प्रिय भरतहि सम भाई॥

Praising You profusely, the king of the Raghu Clan (Sri Rama) said – You are a dear brother to me, just like Bharata.

13. सहस बदन तुम्हरो जस गावैं।
अस कहि श्रीपति कंठ लगावैं॥

"The thousand-faced One (Shesha) sings your praise," saying this, Sri Rama embraced You.

These three verses, and the following two also, relate to a single theme – Hanuman bringing the *Sanjivanee* herb. Going by word count, this is the longest theme in the whole of the Hanuman Chalisa.

Let us see the background that necessitated the presence of the herb. Tulsidas has a slightly different view of the entire incident than what we find in the Valmiki Ramayana. Indrajit shot the *veeraghatini shakti* at Lakshmana, and as a result, He fell down senseless. In the evening, Hanuman saw Him lying on the ground and brought Him to the *Vanara* camp.

Jambavan suggested seeking the help of Sushena, the royal physician of Lanka. Maruti, who by now had become an expert in moving in and out of Lanka, entered the enemy territory in His *laghu rupa*. He brought Sushena along with his entire house, and it is needless to say that He would have done that in His *virat rupa*.

On Sushena's advice, He flew towards the Himalayas to bring the *sanjivanee* herb. On the way, He stopped at a hermitage where the *mayavi* demon Kalanemi was stationed, assuming the guise of a sage. After killing the demon, He finally reached the Himalayas. Failing to recognize the right herb, He brought the entire mountain with Him. On the way back, Hanuman was intercepted by Bharata. After a brief interaction, He returned and delivered the package on time. Lakshmana was revived and brought back to life by Sushena's medicines. An elated Rama expressed His heartfelt gratitude and embraced Hanuman. Hanuman finished the task by carrying Sushena back to his place in Lanka.

Valmiki's story goes like this. Staying invisible in the sky, Indrajit had launched a fierce attack on the Raghava brothers. When he shot the *Brahmastra*, Rama advised Lakshmana to face the arrow without any resistance. The idea was to fool Indrajit – he would take the unconscious brothers as dead and go back from the battlefield. The *astra* had a very devastating impact – all of Rama's associates and soldiers, with the exception of Anjaneya and Vibhishana, fell to the ground, either dead or unconscious. Jambavan and Sugreeva regained consciousness after a while. It was Jambavan and not the Lankan physician Sushena, who suggested the need for the herbs. There were, in fact, four of them - *Mrita Sanjeevani, Vishalyakarani, Souvarnakarani* and

Sandhaani. The names suggest their specific modes of action: reviving back to life, healing wounds, bringing back vitality, and finally healing the broken joints. All of them were available on a mountain peak between two famous trans-Himalayan mountains, Kailasha and Rishabha.

During the onward journey, Veera Anjaneya jumped from the top of the *Trikuta* mountain, on which the city of Lanka was situated, and thence to Mount *Malaya*. From there onwards, He took a leap to cross the ocean. It was His first landing and take-off from within the city limits, and as a result, the gates and buildings of Lanka got shattered.

When He reached the mountain full of herbs, the healing plants made themselves invisible. Time was running out for Hanuman, and He responded by speaking to the presiding spirit of the mountain – "If you have already made up your mind not to show any compassion towards Lord Rama today, then be prepared to get crushed under my hands." Then, He plucked the entire mountain peak and started flying again.

There is no mention of any physician preparing medicine out of the healing plants. Just by smelling their fragrances, the Princes and all the *Vanaras* regained their consciousness.

Interestingly, the amazing herbs worked even on the *Vanaras* who had already died in the preceding days. Naturally, a question arises at this point: why did it not revive the dead rakshasas? Well, even before the war had started, Ravana had issued a directive that the bodies of all the soldiers of his army who died fighting should be thrown into the ocean. This was done with an eye on maintaining the rakshasa-prestige!

There is no mediation of Sushena, the Vaidya from Lanka, nor any mention of Kalanemi or Bharata on the way. Some recensions of the Valmiki Ramayana do contain a reference to the Kalanemi legend, even though the critical edition and the popular southern recension do not. For Valmiki's Hanuman, it was more or less a smooth journey. Surprisingly, there is no mention of Rama embracing Hanuman also. If we read Valmiki's epic, there was actually no time for this formality in that critical hour. On His return journey with the herb-mountain, Hanuman had landed directly on the *Trikuta* mountain. At that point of time, there were only a handful of monkeys along with Vibhishana, to receive Him. All others were lying unconscious under the spell of Brahmastra. A happy Anjaneya embraced Vibhishana on the mountain top. Moreover, He had the responsibility of keeping the piece of mountain back in its place and coming back to the battlefield. He did exactly that before the night was over.

As soon as Hanuman returned from the Himalayas for the second time on that fateful night, Sugreeva had something important to discuss.

The very powerful Kumbhakarna had been killed the previous day. Indrajit had also retired, thinking that he had successfully eliminated his enemies. Until this point, the fight was limited to the battlefield, probably on the seashore and definitely far away from the capital city, which was situated on the mountain top. Sugreeva was keen on taking the fight right onto the residence of Ravana – *ghar me ghus ke marenge* kind of aspiration! He said, "Ravana would not be able to offer resistance. This is the best time to attack. Let us enter the city and set it on fire, without wasting any time."

However odd it looks for the readers of the Valmiki Ramayana to move ahead without a word of appreciation from the Master, there was actually no time for that—the evening had been hectic for the Vayuputra. For some reason, He had decided to take off and land on a mountain away from their base camp; the Master Himself had come under the spell of Brahmastra, and Sugreeva was not ready to waste even a minute in executing his frontal attack on the enemy camp.

Now, the question arises: a grateful Rama embracing a humble Anjaneya is the most prevalent image of the Duo across the subcontinent. How could that happen if Valmiki did not write anything on the very famous thanksgiving-embrace? Well, Rama had actually expressed His gratitude towards Hanuman by embracing Him, but at a different time and location. The famous embracing happened upon the latter's return from Lanka. He was delighted to the core when Hanuman brought the news of Sita. Sri Ramachandra's words were somewhat like this: "Today, my brother and I, and my entire clan, feel that we have been saved by the grace of Dharma. But it pains my heart that I am not able to gift You anything equally precious. Oh, dear Hanuman, You are everything to me. Let me embrace You. At this moment, that is the only thing that I can present to You." This is one of the most potent and emotional statements of the *Ramayana Parampara.* The depth of expression, along with the beautiful Sanskrit poetry had a far-reaching effect in the entire sub-continent and even beyond. All the major regional versions of the Ramayana have further glorified this episode.

This is the precise reason why we see millions of photos and idols depicting Rama-Hanuman embracing each other.

There are many instances in the Ramayana, where Lord Rama has declared that Bharata is the dearest to Him among the Raghava brothers. When Vibhishana defected and came to the *Vanara* camp, no one except Maruti argued in his favour. Everyone believed that his animosity towards Ravana was fake. Then Sri Rama explained to Sugreeva, "Not all families stay happy and united; differences do arise. His difference with Ravana looks genuine to me. O dear Sugreeva, not all brothers are like Bharata - न सर्वे भ्रातरस्तात भवन्ति भरतोपमाः".

Raghupati, for sure, spoke very highly about Anjaneya. In the *Ramcharitmanas*, He says, "There is no God, sage or human being more helpful than You – *sunu kapi tohi samana upakari, nahi kou sura nara muni tanudhari*". The occasions may have been different, but Raghupati never shied away from expressing His gratitude towards Anjaneya. Similarly, He may not have uttered the exact words *Tuma mama priya Bharata hi sama bhai* in *Ramcharitmanas*, but He has spoken similar and even greater things elsewhere. For example, when Hanuman met Him for the first time and assured Him of all help from Sugreeva's side, a grateful Raghava extolled, "Tai mama priya Lachimana te duna – You are twice as dear to me as Lakshmana is". And Rama had used this expression "You are as dear to me as Bharata is" for Sugreeva when he came to the Lord to inform Him that the search for Sita had already begun.

The word *Sahasavadana* is interpreted as "one with a thousand faces". While it could mean praising someone repeatedly or being praised by thousands of people, it also refers to Shesha, the thousand-headed serpent holding the Earth. After Hanuman's return from Lanka, Jambavan took Him to Sri Rama and said, "O Lord, even a thousand voices cannot narrate the accomplishments of Hanuman - नाथ पवनसुत कीन्हि जो करनी। सहसहुँ मुख न जाइ सो बरनी ॥."

However, Lakshmana was an incarnation of Shesha, and there is every reason to believe that at that particular point of time, both Rama and Lakshmana were continuing with their admiration for Hanuman. A very interesting thing to note here is the use of the word *Shripati* for Lord Rama. If we take the literal meaning, it translates to "the Husband of Lakshmi Devi". We all know that Lakshmi, Narayana, and Shesha are a unit, and that makes Lakshmana, as the interpretation of the word *Sahasavadana*, more appropriate.

These three verses speak about the relationship between Raghupati and Hanuman, and the high regard the former had for the latter. Continuing with the same spirit, the *Chalisa* narrates how the entire universe sings the praise of the ultimate *veera, bhakta* and *jnani* and still feels it could have sung more.

14. सनकादिक ब्रह्मादि मुनीसा।
नारद सारद सहित अहीसा॥

15. जम कुबेर दिगपाल जहाँ ते।
कबि कोबिद कहि सकैं कहाँ ते॥

Sanaka and the sages, Lord Brahma and other Gods, Sage Narada, Devi Sarasvati, Shesha, Yama, Kuvera, and other Guardians of the directions – none can sing your glory enough; what to speak of poets and scholars!

This is a list of divinities who sing the glories of Hanuman. When we start analysing a little, two patterns emerge from the list. Sanaka, Sanandana, Sanatana and Sanat Kumara are the four mind - born sons of Lord Brahma. Narada Muni is also another mind-born son of the Lord of Creation. Devi Sarasvati is His wife. *Brahma loka* is believed to be situated on *Nakapristham,* or the top of the heaven. Our tradition places the abode of Lord Brahma in the galaxy at the highest point above the Earth. Shesha, the serpent, is located below the Earth. *Dikpalas* are four – Indra, Yama, Varuna and Kuvera, protecting the eastern, southern, western and northern directions, respectively. From an astronomical perspective, they collectively cover all the four cardinal directions and the space above and below the Earth. The idea latent in the verse sums up the entire conceivable universe.

The second pattern is about hierarchy. Thousands of sages are mentioned in our scriptures, but the status of Sanaka and His brothers is the highest among all. Lord Brahma is accepted as the supreme among the Devas. Narada Muni is the greatest among the devotees of Lord Vishnu. Devi Sarasvati stands for *Vak* or speech, and the Vedas celebrate Her status above everyone and everything. Shesha is the supreme serpent, the only one to have been offered the status of a God. Guardians of the directions are sovereign masters of their own kingdoms. In other words, this verse is a list of the topmost ones from different groups of divine beings.

The *Mahaviri Vyakhya* interprets the word *Ahisha* as either Lord Vishnu, who reclines on Shesha, or Lord Mahadeva, who adorns a serpent. Swamiji's point is that Shesha has just been mentioned as *Sahasavadana* in the previous verse, so it is logical to interpret *Ahi* as Shesha and *Ahisha* (*Isha of Ahi* or Lord of the Serpent) as the master of Shesha, i.e., Lord Vishnu or Shiva.

In a nutshell, Goswami ji wants to convey that the glory of Hanuman ji is popular across the universe, and His greatness is endorsed by the greatest of the greats. When they all cannot eulogize Him enough, how can a human brain think of putting His fame into words!

16. तुम उपकार सुग्रीवहिं कीन्हा।
राम मिलाय राजपद दीन्हा॥

You did a great help to Sugreeva. You introduced him to Rama and gave him kingship.

This one and the following verse speak of how Hanuman was a king-maker in the Ramayana. He made Sugreeva a king by introducing him to Sri Rama. But He just arranged a meeting between the two heroes - what was so special about that? The Raghava brothers had been directed by the demon Kavandha to meet Sugreeva. They were broadly aware of his address on the *Rishyamuka* mountain, and They would have met him in any case! Or it was not just a simple "**introduction**" as it seems – let's see!

Vali had been cursed to stay away from the mountain, but, despite this, Sugreeva was living under constant fear in those days. Both the Valmiki Ramayana and the *Ramcharitmanas* have used adjectives like *ati sabheeta* and *parama bheeta* to describe Sugreeva's state of mind. The moment the brothers appeared within the *Vanaras*' visual range, many of them started fleeing from their mountain abode, and even Sugreeva was about to follow- *Pathae Vali hohin man maila, bhaagon turat tajo yaha shailaa.*

All this happened when the brothers had just reached the foothill, far away from Sugreeva's actual residence.

There was very little chance that he would have agreed to meet Them had the Brothers approached independently.

And then enters everyone's favourite character, Maruti, with His opening statement - संभ्रमः त्यजताम् – "Give up your confusion!" This is so typical of Him, reassuring someone when he needs it the most. He continues – "This is *Rishyamuka* mountain; Vali just cannot enter this place, and he is nowhere to be seen". During this conversation, Hanuman addresses Sugreeva as "Raja" – "O Sugreeva, you are a king. Your knowledge and confidence must be reflected in your body language."

For Him, Sugreeva was always a king. How could He not have put all His efforts into bringing back Sugreeva's kingship?

At Sugreeva's behest, He took the guise of an ascetic and went down the mountain to meet the brothers. He had a short conversation, inquiring about their identity and the purpose of their visit to that lonely forest.

We have no idea how long this conversation went on, but what we know is that it left a lifelong impression on the Raghava brothers about the capability of Hanuman. Rama just could not stop narrating the charm of Anjaneya; His knowledge of the Vedas, His hold on grammar, His voice modulation, choice of words, confidence, tone, and everything about Him was so mesmerizing! This statement is the epitome of Sri Rama's appreciation for Hanuman - "He talks so nicely that even an enemy with a raised sword would start loving Him! (कस्य न आराध्यते चित्तम् उद्यत् असे अरेः अपि)"

After this brief account, Lakshmana started conversing with Hanuman. Even before meeting Sugreeva, Lakshmana assured the Vayuputra that they would help the king-in-exile as per His wish. The victory for Sugreeva was sealed even before the actual meeting took place, and the entire credit goes to Hanuman. The physical meeting that followed was but a formality.

A significant difference lies between the description of both the sides in the Tulasi and Valmiki Ramayanas. In the *Ramcharitmanas*, Hanuman speaks of Sugreeva as Sri Rama's *Dasa* and requests the brothers to make him free of fear. Just contrary to this, Valmiki's Lakshmana says – "We both have come to the shelter of the Vanara King; we accept his lordship!" Hanuman assures them, on behalf of Sugreeva, that they all would help the brothers in finding the lost Princess.

Then He takes both the brothers and introduces Them to an anxious Sugreeva. And what an introduction it was!

Maruti takes a three-step approach. First, He describes Rama as *Dridha Vikrama* and *Satya Vikrama*. Then, He tells Sugreeva that the two brothers have come to his refuge. And He further makes a strong recommendation to accept their friendship and honour them - एतौ पूजनीयतमौ उभौ - He describes the brothers as the two most worthy of receiving veneration.

Let us see the sense that the three short sentences spoken by Anjaneya reflect.

Step One. *Sri Rama's valour is resolute and firm; He would be a worthy ally. He has the ability to remove your sufferings. Truth is His valour; if He makes a promise to get your kingdom back, think it to be done. He will never step back.*

With this, He ignited a spark of hope in the depressed king.

Step Two. *Although being very strong, these two brothers are entirely harmless. In fact, they have come to your refuge. They are seeking your help.*

In step two, He dispelled all fear and anxiety from Sugreeva's mind and brought him to normalcy from an agitated state so that he could understand the two brothers as gifts of destiny standing before him.

Step Three. *They have come here seeking your friendship. My assessment says that they are not just princes from a renowned clan or strong warriors. They belong to the highest category of human beings, the best among those who are worthy of worship. I strongly recommend that you accept and honour Them.*

In step three, He made a strong case for the alliance to happen.

Hanuman ji spoke on behalf of both the sides, narrated the story of each side to the other, and forged a very strong friendship between them. He was continuing with His ascetic form and came back to His *Vanara rupa* only after Rama and Sugreeva accepted and embraced each other. He kindled the fire and both of them circumambulated. The friends took a pledge: "from now onwards, your pain and pleasure are mine, and mine are yours." (एकम् दुःखम् सुखम् च नौ)

The alliance was forged with Anjaneya's guarantee, and He was the sole architect of it. He formalised it by keeping *Agni* as the witness.

So, this was His style of "**introducing**" Sugreeva to Ram ji.

17. तुम्हरो मंत्र बिभीषन माना।
लंकेश्वर भए सब जग जाना॥

The whole world knows that Vibhishana became the king of Lanka by following Your motto.

The *Mahaviri Vyakhya* has a beautiful analogy to explain these two verses. Hanuman ji connected two great souls with the Prabhu. He carried Lord Rama to Sugreeva's place and led Vibhishana to the Lord. He did so by narrating Sri Rama's "prabhaav" to Sugreeva and explaining His "swabhaav" to Vibhishana.

The Valmiki Ramayana does not give any details of Hanuman meeting Vibhishana in Lanka. However, He had heard very positive things about Vibhishana and his family from Sita, and had seen him pleading with Ravana to free the Princess from captivity. And that was the reason He spared Vibhishana's house while setting the city on fire.

Valmiki's portrayal of characters is always very practical, and every person appears to be multi-faceted when seen through his lens.

Valmiki's Vibhishana, in addition to being a kind person with high moral values, also had a desire to be the king of Lanka. Vibhishana had lamented that his dream of achieving the kingship of Lanka was shattered when the two brothers got injured by Indrajit's serpent-weapon. Except for this lamentation, there is no overt expression in the text to support the view. But we see a glimpse of this aspect of Vibhishana during the conversation between Hanuman and Rama, which took place when Vibhishana left Lanka to seek the Lord's refuge. When everybody else in the Vanara camp was reluctant to accept Ravana's brother, Hanuman enumerated a number of reasons as to why Vibhishana might have come to seek refuge. The list included Rama's enterprise, Ravana's falsehood, the news of Vali's death and the subsequent coronation of Sugreeva. Hanuman concluded His statement by saying that Vibhishana's aspiration for the kingdom could also have been a reason for his arrival. And as per the text, even Rama had endorsed Hanuman's view at that point.

It seems to be against the spirit of Vibhishana's dedication because, unlike Sugreeva, he had never expressed his intention for the throne publicly. By all probability, he would have continued serving his elder brother had there been no abduction of Sita.

Then what could have been the mantra that Valmiki's Vibhishana received from Anjaneya?

It is very much possible that Vibhishana was impressed by the Rama-Hanuman relationship built on trust and devotion. The *saatvik* persona within him must have aspired to be a selfless associate of the Lord, just like Hanuman. He saw a *Vanara* who crossed the ocean and killed a portion of the enemy army all by Himself. Still, when the need arose, the Vanara chose to tolerate unspeakable humiliation, and even allowed fire to be set to His tail, just to ensure that His Master would have a smoother victory march in the future. All these things must have inspired Vibhishana to shift his loyalty.

But, Goswamiji's Vibhishana is an out-and-out bhakta. In the *Ramcharitmanas*, Hanuman assumes the form of a *Vipra* and goes on to meet him. When the Lankan hero laments on his *tamasic* body, Hanuman consoles him with words and says, "Look at me. Do I look like someone from a very high lineage? I am but an ape."

Vibhishana was already a great devotee of Sri Rama, but he did not have the hope that the Lord would bless him ever. Meeting with Hanuman strengthened his resolve, particularly after listening to the words – "Listen, O Vibhishana. Loving His servants has always been the style of my Master" (*sunahu Vibhishana prabhu ke riti, karahi sada sevak para priti*).

Considering the revengeful attitude of his brother, Vibhishana's defection was a great leap. In the normal course, he would have decided to stay back in Lanka even after facing repeated humiliations from Ravana. However, following the motto of Hanuman changed his destiny, both politically and spiritually. In Swami

Rambhadracharyaji's words, it got him both "Rama pada" and "Raja pada".

Sri Rama asked Lakshmana to fetch water from the ocean and consecrate Vibhishana as the king of Lanka. This happened immediately after he came to Sri Rama's refuge. A prince-in-exile, staying as an ascetic, consecrated the brother-turned-enemy of the most powerful king on Earth. The ritual did not happen at some secret location; it happened right on the seashore when the whole world was watching. When such a thing happens, the world keeps track till its fruition. And finally, when Vibhishana ascended the throne, the entire world acknowledged in unison.

18. जुग सहस्र जोजन पर भानू।
लील्यो ताहि मधुर फल जानू॥

The Sun was two thousand yojanas away. You thought it to be a sweet fruit and grabbed it.

This very famous legend of Hanuman's childhood has come down to us in many different versions. The most popular one is a combination of multiple versions. It says that infant Hanuman once felt hungry. When He saw the rising Sun, He thought it to be an edible fruit and took a leap to have it. An anxious Indra struck His Vajra on the child. Under the impact of the Vajra, infant Hanuman fell down unconscious on a mountain top with a broken jaw. His father, the Wind God, protested at this and stopped blowing. The entire universe came to a standstill. Led by Lord Brahma, all the Devas reached the spot. To their surprise, the kid was doing well even after the fall. Then, the divine blessings were literally poured on the kid. His jaw was fixed; He was blessed with immunity from all kinds of assaults, and all the Devas granted Him their own strength. As the kid's jawbone or "hanu" was broken, He was named Hanuman.

The most debatable word in the verse is "Juga". Though a large section of readers and devotees take this as "Yuga", some beg to differ. *Yuga,* in Indian tradition, is a measure of time. There is no consensus on the definition of *yuga*, but the most commonly held view is that of 12,000 years. *Yojana* is a measure of distance, ranging from 8 to 15 kilometers in today's standard. Approximately 8 miles or 12.8 kilometers is the most commonly accepted magnitude of a *yojana*. If we take *Sahasra* as one thousand, then the distance of the Sun from Hanuman's place becomes 12,000 × 1,000 × 12.8 kilometers or 15,36,00,000 kilometers. This is really very close to the actual distance of 15,14,07,000 kilometers!

This incredible precision puts the authenticity of our ancient knowledge on a very high pedestal, but there is a little confusion here. Goswami ji has used the word "Juga" and not "Yuga". *Juga* in the *Ramcharitmanas* conveys a sense of a pair, such as joining "both" hands in prayer or the "two" letters of the *Rama nama,* and so on. And even if we take it as *Yuga*, why should a unit that measures time be used to convey a sense of distance? Similarly, *sahasra yojana* may be construed as thousands and thousands of *yojanas* in a broad sense and not exactly a thousand *yojanas*.

Project Shivoham, a very popular channel on YouTube, describes it in an interesting way. When the infant Anjaneya grabbed Surya Deva, He and the star became one for that moment. *Yuga* or *Juga* stands for that oneness rather than a measure of distance.

A reader's attention is drawn to two more questions here. Did Hanuman actually grab the Sun? And did His famous name derive from His broken jaw?

The Valmiki Ramayana holds the answer to the questions. It specifically mentions that even after travelling for three hundred *yojanas*, Maruti felt no fatigue. Indra struck His vajra when He saw the child approaching the *antariksha* very fast. In our tradition, *antariksha* is mid-way between Earth and heaven, and certainly very far from the vault or "Naaka" where the Sun stays.

Of course, this does not mean that He was struck down exactly at a distance of 300 yojanas from the Earth. We do not actually know how close He was to the Sun when He fell down on a mountain top, but He was flying very fast, and by all probability, He would have reached the Sun soon.

Tulsidas, however, maintains that Maruti had grabbed the star thinking it to be a sweet fruit. *Sankata Mochan Hanumanashtaka*, also a famous prayer of eight verses by Goswami ji, explicitly mentions the Sun being swallowed by Hanuman *(baal samay Ravi bhaksh liyo).*

Now, let us examine the impact of the Vajra strike on infant Hanuman.

The story of Hanuman getting charged up by the speech of Jambavan is a very famous one. During this conversation, Jambavan narrates the episode of infant Hanuman getting struck by the Vajra. The exact verse in the *Kishkindha Kanda* is – तदा शैलाग्र शिखरे वामो हनुर् अभज्यत | ततो हि नाम धेयम् ते हनुमान् इति कीर्तितम् – and the popular translation would be "Then, your left jaw bone was broken on the mountain top and from thence Your name became famous as Hanuman". But this is not as straightforward as it looks. The *Mahaviri Vyakhya* says "Abhajyata" in Sanskrit can come from two roots – "Bhanj" or to break, and "Bhaj" or to serve and honour.

If we move just three verses ahead in the same Valmiki Ramayana, we encounter a line that says Hanuman was completely unhurt from the impact of Vajra - वज्रस्य च निपातेन विरुजम् त्वाम् समीक्ष्य च. "Man" is a suffix used for someone when He is blessed with something impressive or spectacular. For example, we call a man *buddhiman* when we believe that he is intelligent in a good way. Why should someone with a broken jaw be called Hanuman, even if the defect was repaired immediately? Or was He named so because the bone was successfully repaired?

If we take the entire chapter into account, then Hanuman was never hurt; He just fell down. *Vajra* did not break His jaw. Instead, it paid its respect to something even stronger than itself. And the name Hanuman must have come from "someone having a jaw stronger than the *Vajra*" and not "one with a broken-and-repaired jaw". This is further attested in the millions of Hanuman idols sculpted across centuries, none of which show Him with a broken jawbone.

Anjaneya is very popular among the tribals, and there is a fascinating folklore related to this episode in the Munda tradition. When infant Hanuman was travelling fast to catch hold of the Sun, the *Devas* thought of protecting Him from the impact of extreme heat. To distract the kid, they donned colourful dresses and decorative masks and started dancing on the ground. The kid was attracted by the dance and the sound of loud music, and came down to join them. What ensued was a divine dance with spectacular dresses. People surrounding the place took note of the steps and thus began the very famous *Chhau* dance. In his essay on "Adivasi lok jivan mein Hanuman ji" published in the special issue of the Kalyan magazine, Sri Sunil Kumar gives a beautiful narration of the folklore.

19. प्रभु मुद्रिका मेलि मुख माहीं।
जलधि लाँघि गये अचरज नाहीं॥

No wonder You crossed the ocean, keeping the Lord's ring in Your mouth.

Continuing with the theme of the second quarter, Goswami ji writes about another flight of the Vayuputra. This time, He crossed the ocean effortlessly, carrying the ring of His master. This ease or effortlessness is the theme of this verse. Needless to say, the blessings of Rama and His own supreme power were the keys to His success.

Let us see the background of the event in the *Ramcharitmanas*.

The search for Sita had begun, and the *Vanara* party was leaving Kishkindha. As a mark of respect, all of them were taking Sri Rama's blessings before proceeding on their respective routes. Anjaneya was the last one in the queue. Knowing well that He would accomplish the task, Sri Rama asked Anjaneya to come near Him. The Raghu Prince gently placed His hands on Anjaneya's head and gave Him the signet ring as a recognition of being the greatest *Rama Bhakta*.

The *Ramcharitmanas* does not tell us about Hanuman keeping the ring inside His mouth. Nor is He known to have done this before taking the leap to cross the ocean. *Gitavali*, another famous composition of Goswami ji, does, however, contain a suggestive verse. The first line of the fifth chapter tells us that when Hanuman received His Master's signet ring along with orders to proceed, He opened His mouth (to keep the ring inside) and bowed down His head happily (and departed)– *Rajaayasu Ram ko jab payo, gaal meli Mudrika, mudita mana Pavanasuta sir naayo. Gitavali's* "gaal" has been replaced by "mukh" in the *Chalisa*. Catherine Ludvik thinks that upon receiving the token of Rama's identity, Maruti kissed it rather than keeping it inside His mouth. The idea was to imprint the Lord's name on His lips.

And this makes sense, because both the *Chalisa* and *Gitavali* simply wish to convey the message that *Rama Nama*, inscribed on the ring, got permanently imprinted on Maruti's lips. Flying across the ocean was the first major task accomplished by Hanuman with His master's blessings – it shaped His destiny for all time to come. Putting the ring on the lips or inside the mouth is a symbolic presentation of Anjaneya's initiation in *Rama Nama*, and undoubtedly, He was the first ever disciple to be initiated in this *Parampara*.

As regards the flight over the ocean, it was not entirely uneventful. Hanuman had three encounters: one overtly friendly with the Mainaka Mountain, another a seemingly difficult but friendly and affectionate one in reality, with Surasa, and a purely hostile one that happened with the demoness Simhika. We see a glimpse of Hanuman's politeness in dealing with Mainaka Mountain. All the grateful mountain wanted was a short break journey and a little relaxation for Anjaneya. Anjaneya reciprocated by just touching the surface of the mountain and flying up again. Surasa was the mother of the Nagas. Her intention was to test the capabilities of Hanuman. She created a barrier by enlarging herself to a gigantic proportion. The respectful *Vanara* also expanded Himself, then assumed a miniature form, entered her mouth, and came out with lightning speed. In the third encounter, He had to give up His civility and engage in a real fight. Assuming the same strategy, He entered Simhika's mouth but came out only after tearing apart her vital organs.

Though words like *kautuka* and *leela* have been used in the *Ramcharitmanas* to describe Anjaneya's effortlessness in accomplishing the task, Goswamiji's actual aim is to glorify the power of *Rama Bhakti* in the success of the mission.

In contrast, Valmiki's portrayal of the entire event has a lot of nuances.

When Sugreeva was instructing all the *Vanaras* to begin the search for Sita, Raghava was sitting nearby. He saw Sugreeva talking to many of them, but the conversation with Hanuman was something special. Not only was Sugreeva confident that Anjaneya would accomplish the task, but even Anjaneya's face was beaming with self-confidence. Raghava thought – "This man looks like the chosen one among Sugreeva's emissaries. A king will talk like this to someone only when his track record is very impressive". Sri Rama started feeling that the job was almost done.

Then, a delighted Raghava asked Hanuman to come near Him and gave Him a ring engraved with His own name. Rama did not give the ring under the spell of emotion. He did a critical analysis of Sugreeva-Hanuman conversation and decided to give the ring only when He became very sure of Hanuman's success.

Hanuman received the ring, placed it on His own head, touched the feet of the Lord with folded hands, and began to depart (स तत् गृह्य हरिश्रेष्ठः स्थाप्य मूर्ध्नि कृतांजलिः).

So, the ring was placed on the "Head" (could have been tied to or embedded within His curly hairs) and not within the "Mouth". स्थाप्य मूर्ध्नि has been replaced with मेलि मुख माहीं – head replaced with mouth!

However, one thing remains unanswered. If writing did not exist in ancient India, how could Rama's ring be engraved with His name? And if it existed, what script was being used during that time?

In the academic circle, two completely opposite views exist on this episode. Scholars like H D Sankalia and Catherine Ludvik believe that signet rings were introduced into North-Western India by the Greeks in the 1st century BCE, and hence, this legend has to be a later interpolation into the Valmiki Ramayana. They have suggested the 2nd century CE as the time of this interpolation when the original composition was expanding, giving rise to vulgate editions. On the other hand, Lutgendorf thinks that Hanuman handing over the ring to Sita is the seed or *beej* from which the entire epic of Ramayana has grown.

For all practical purposes, the questions remain unanswered.

If the Prince had chosen to keep the ring with Him even during the forest-exile, it must have been priceless for Him. And handing it over to someone who was supposed to embark on a difficult journey across the ocean speaks of Rama's trust in Hanuman.

20. दुर्गम काज जगत के जेते।
सुगम अनुग्रह तुम्हरे तेते ॥

All the difficult tasks of this world become easy with Your grace.

The saga of the three famous flights of Hanuman ends with the previous verse. And this verse ends the second quarter.

The theme is obvious.

A curriculum vitae of the Deva has been built. All the remarkable achievements and appreciations of the divine master of crisis management have been narrated. The poet wants to assure the devotee that Maruti's blessing is enough to carry him through obstacles, both material and spiritual.

ॐ

SECTION IV
Verses 21 to 30

The third quarter deals with two themes. It projects our Hanuman ji as the closest and dearest associate of Prabhu Rama. Even though Rama is the highest divinity, all His jobs are managed by Hanuman alone. Secondly, it tells us how the grace of Hanuman can confer happiness of all kinds and protection from evil spirits and diseases.

Knowing very well that these material aspirations are but a means to the highest goal, Tulsidas speaks of Hanumanji's ability to bless with things even higher than these.

21. राम दुआरे तुम रखवारे।
होत न आज्ञा बिनु पैसारे॥

You are the guardian of Rama's door. No one enters without Your permission.

However transparent this verse may seem, it is a multi-layered imagery.

From a physical sense, it seems very much practical that during the march to Lanka and throughout the entire duration of the war, Hanuman would have zealously guarded the Raghava brothers. By all probability, He would have continued doing the same even after their return to Ayodhya.

In the spiritual plane, a devotee usually seeks bhakti and *siddhis,* and both of these can be bestowed upon by

Hanuman ji. When a *sadhaka* rises above the average level and starts aspiring for the highest abode of Lord Vishnu, *siddhis* seem immaterial to him. Even that can be achieved through Hanumanji's grace. In fact, the road to the highest abode passes through the Vayuputra.

The third imagery is related to temple iconography. Even Divinities other than Rama look for Hanuman's protection at the entrance to their temples. He is the all-time favourite of Sita-Rama, and His presence at the entrance of their temple is understandable, but how come the entire pantheon of Sanatan divinities seek Anjaneya's protection? There is no definite answer to this question, but scholars believe this is related to the foundation of Hanuman worship in remote antiquity. Some argue in favour of Anjaneya being an indigenous deity who was present among the masses as a protector God. With the advent of Vedic and post-Vedic Hinduism, the cult of Hanuman was incorporated into the mainstream. He belonged to the class of *Yakshas* who protected temples and other important places. No wonder this super-Deity was entrusted with the security of villages, temples and even kingdoms.

22. सब सुख लहै तुम्हारी सरना।
तुम रक्षक काहू को डरना॥

Happiness of all kinds is achieved when one takes refuge in You. With You as the protector, the devotee need not fear anyone.

Hanuman ji offers protection from all outward disturbances. In addition to this, He ensures that the seeker is always happy and content from within. The word *sab sukh* should be interpreted as peace of mind and spiritual enlightenment, more than material pleasure.

This verse is a continuation of the previous one, as they together form the eleventh *chaupai*. The overall sense of these two verses can be summed up as follows: Hanuman is the guardian of Sri Rama's abode. One cannot just enter the place without His permission. But when a devotee with a pure heart seeks His blessings, He not only fulfils the *sadhaka's* wish of meeting Sri Rama, He also takes care of the all-round protection of the person.

23. आपन तेज सम्हारो आपै।
तीनौं लोक हाँक ते काँपै॥

You alone can withstand Your radiance. The three worlds tremble at Your roar.

Anjaneya's strength and valour are matchless in the three worlds. No weapon can touch Him; no spell can confound Him. He has the power to increase or decrease His body size to incredible proportions. He has the blessings of Lords Brahma, Vishnu and Mahadev. Lord Indra has granted Him immunity from all kinds of weapons. He has completed His education under the direct guidance of Surya Deva. And most importantly, He is blessed with *svachhanda mrityu.*

All these attributes make Him an unmatched hero in the universe.

And the whole world witnessed how the one-man army of Hanuman devastated the enemy camp with His bare hands. The *Sundara Kanda* narrates His one-of-a-kind battle skills. Even the Mahabharata tells us about His presence on Arjuna's flag. The mighty Kaurava camp struggled to withstand His wild roar from the chariot top. No wonder the three worlds start trembling when Veera Anjaneya shouts His war cry.

24. भूत पिशाच निकट नहिं आवै।
महाबीर जब नाम सुनावै॥

Evil spirits do not dare to come near when they hear the name of Hanuman ji.

This verse continues with the essence of the previous *chaupai,* that the devotees of Maruti do not have to fear anyone. When the entire universe trembles at His roar, what to speak of *bhutas* and *pishachas*!

Though commonly taken as evil spirits, both these groups have minor differences. *Bhutas* are spirits of dead people; *pishachas* need not have that origin. And while we do not know anything about the food preferences of *bhutas*, *pishachas* thrive on flesh.

The particular emphasis on Hanuman's grace to get rid of *bhutas* and *pishachas* probably stems from two traditions. As per the Shiva Purana and various other Shaiva texts, Hanuman is *Rudravatara*, an *amsha* of Mahadeva. Tulsidas himself has talked about the Shaiva origin of Anjaneya in many of his writings. Therefore, being an *avatara* of *Bhuta-Natha*, He has natural dominance over the spirits. They will stay away from His devotees for sure.

Secondly, "Mahavira" is a tantric title, and during the practice of tantra, Hanuman as the Mahavira ensures complete protection of the devotees from the disturbance caused by these evil elements. The *Agastya Samhita* is considered an authority on the rituals of *Rama upasana*. The thirty-second chapter contains a conversation between Agastya Muni and Suteekshna, in which the celebrated sage Agastya has outlined the details of worshipping Hanuman ji in the tantric system. Recitation of the *tantrik mantra* brings both material comfort and liberation, and evil spirits run away just at the sight of the reciter. Needless to say, this mantra owes its efficacy to the grace of Mahadeva.

Apart from these two theories, there is another interesting account of Hanuman's connection with *Pishachas* in the *Brahma Purana*. Along with Anjana, another *apsara* named Adrika was also cursed to take birth in the mortal world. While Anjana had the face of a *Vanara*, she had that of a cat or *Marjara*. Both were married to Keshari and, in due course of time, gave birth to Hanuman and Adri, respectively. Adri had been born out of the grace of Nirrti and went on to become the king of the *Pishachas*. And this makes Hanuman and Adri half-brothers. The purana also tells us that Adri and Anjaneya helped each other's mothers to get rid of their curses by making them visit sacred *tirthas* on the Godavari.

This role of Hanuman as the protector from evil spirits is best exemplified by His form of Balaji at Mehandipur, Rajasthan. Thousands of devotees throng this famous temple to get rid of spells from *bhutas* and *pishachas*. And very interestingly, Adri, the cousin of Anjaneya, is also worshipped there as *Pretraj Sarkar*.

25. नासै रोग हरै सब पीरा।
जपत निरंतर हनुमत बीरा॥

Constant recitation of the name of Hanuman ji destroys diseases and removes pain of all kinds.

Being the eradicator of diseases and suffering is one of the most popular aspects of Lord Hanuman. Millions of devotees chant His name to regain health and happiness.

But Hanuman Himself is no physician! Then, how did this epithet come to be associated with Him?

Well, He is not a trained physician for sure, but He successfully brought the herbs that saved Lakshmana's life. In fact, there were four different herbs - *Mrita Sanjeevani*, *Vishalyakarani*, *Souvarnakarani* and *Sandhaani*. As the names suggest, they were a complete package and worked by restoring life, healing wounds caused by sharp weapons, increasing vitality and healing fractured bones, respectively. The trans-Himalayan herbs were so powerful that they cured Lakshmana and brought back His consciousness in a matter of seconds. Not only that, they cured all the injured *Vanaras* and even revived all the dead *Vanaras*, who had died fighting with the demons, back to life. What a spectacular achievement!

Even during the first deadly attack from Indrajit, Hanuman was supposed to get the herbs *Sanjivakaranee* and *Vishalyaa* from the *milk ocean*. As we have seen earlier, the Valmiki Ramayana does not speak about Sushena, the royal physician of Lanka. But it does speak about Sushena, the *Vanara* and the father-in-law of Sugreeva. It was *Vanara* Sushena who had suggested these herbs. However, Garuda came to the help of the Raghava brothers and the job was done.

Having the abilities to offer protection from evil spirits and to destroy disease and pain have one link in common– the blessings of Mahadeva. As Hanuman ji is an *amsha* of Lord Shiva, such things come naturally to Him. At one end, Mahadeva is "*Bhuta-Natha*", the Lord of all the *Bhutas*, and at the other end, He is "*Bhishajaam Bhishaktamam*" or the best among the physicians, as per the Rig Veda. When we take a composite view of verses 24 and 25, we see *Rudra Rupa* Hanuman.

Diseases and pain need not only be physical; they can be mental or even spiritual. Our Anjaneya removes pain and deformities (*klesha vikara*), guards against evil thoughts (*kumati nivara*), wards off evil spirits (*bhuta pishacha nikata nahi ave*), and destroys diseases and pain (*nashe roga hare sab pira*).

But there is a rider – the chanting has to be uninterrupted; or in other words, the surrender onto Him has to be complete!

The following verse deals with this precondition in more details.

26. संकट तें हनुमान छुड़ावै।
मन क्रम बचन ध्यान जो लावै॥

Hanuman ji protects him from crisis, whoever focuses his thoughts, actions and speech on Him.

This should be interpreted in continuation with the preceding verses of the third quarter. *Pavanasuta* has a splendid track record as a crisis manager for His master. And as a God staying amongst us, He is naturally protective of all His devotees. All the obstacles mentioned before, such as diseases, evil spirits and fear of any kind, can create a crisis in our worldly as well as spiritual life. Hanuman ji is the go-to Deity for all such situations. All He expects in return is the immersion of our entire being in His devotion.

Mana-krama-vachana, meaning thought-action-speech, is a group of words commonly found in the

Ramcharitmanas. It is one of those signature-styles of Goswami ji. It carries the connotation that somebody's mind, body and speech are in perfect unison. There is complete honesty in his thoughts, which gets reflected in his actions and speech. This expression also has the feeling of "the entire being", the *kaya-mano-vakya*.

The presence of the word "*Dhyana*", particularly after "*mana-krama-vachana*", is very significant here. We may use the word "*dhyana*" loosely to mean meditation or contemplation, but in reality, it is a step in *Yoga sadhana* to attain self-realization.

Dharana is the practice of keeping the mind steady and focused on a single point. *Dhyana* comes after *Dharana* in the eight-step yoga or *Ashtanga Yoga*. It is said to have happened when a single uninterrupted beam of thought is directed towards the object of *dharana*. The word *nirantara* in the previous verse (together, they make one *chaupai*) signifies this uninterruptedness conveyed by *dhyana* here.

But if that is the case, then it raises a serious question.

Dhyana is essentially an activity of the mind, so how do we do *dhyana* through speech and action?

Well, there could be two possibilities. It could mean conducting oneself in a way that pleases God, which involves speaking the right words and doing the right things. And it could also mean a continuous and wholehearted surrender to God that covers every sphere of our existence, including speech and action. The poet of the *Chalisa* is talking about a state of constant and complete union with Him – *Let nothing in me remain which is not focused towards Hanuman ji.*

The path of self-realization is full of surprises, and no one manages the crisis better than *Sankata-Mochana Hanuman*. But His grace needs three prerequisites: all we think in our **mana** should be directed towards Ram ji (*Jnana Yoga*), all the **karma** that we perform should be offered to the Lord (*Karma Yoga*) and every word we speak in our **vachana** should sing the unblemished fame of Raghuvara (*Bhakti Yoga*).

Self-realization is the objective of the poet, which is made very clear at the beginning of the *Chalisa*. In this verse, he reinforces his commitment and seeks Maruti's blessings to attain the highest stage in Yoga.

27. सब पर राम तपस्वी राजा।
तिन के काज सकल तुम साजा॥

The ascetic king Rama is the highest among all. All His tasks are carried out by You.

The second part of the verse is straightforward in its meaning - Ram ji gets all His works done through Hanuman. Ever since they met, The Son of Anjana took charge of all the responsibilities of the Lord. Getting the whereabouts of Sita Ma, leading the *Vanara* troupe to Lanka, fighting the war, bringing the lifesaving herbs to revive Lakshmana - the Ramayana is full of such illustrations. This unique relationship probably continued even after Rama's return to Ayodhya.

But what is a bit puzzling is the interpretation of the first part. Translated into simple English, it means the ascetic king Rama is above all others.

We may interpret *Tapasvi Raja* as The One who is both an ascetic and a king, or the ascetic among kings, or the king of ascetics. In fact, all three interpretations fit into Sri Rama's persona.

The relative superiority of Rama can have a multi-layered meaning. Being the king-to-be of Ayodhya, He was the natural first citizen of the kingdom. He might have been staying in the forest, but Bharata was only managing the kingdom as His representative. Secondly, the forest also belonged to the kingdom of Ayodhya. So, technically speaking, the forest-dwelling ascetic Rama was still the king. Therefore, whether in the forest or the capital, Sri Rama had always been the first citizen.

But Tulsidas was not talking of the historical Rama alone. He could never confine his Lord to the role of an ascetic and a king. Centuries before his time, a standalone cult of Sri Rama had already been established. He was a *Ramanandi*; deeply ingrained within the philosophy of this sect is Raghunatha's status as the *Parama Brahma*. Then how could the *Chalisa* not have declared the ascetic king as above everyone!

Comprehending The Supreme Soul is not within everyone's capacity. Where does He stay, how does He look – all these are beyond the mental capability of an average human being. But Hanuman continues to live on this planet, very much among us. For Tulsidas and millions of devotees, He is the recognizable face of the *Parama Brahma*!

**28. और मनोरथ जो कोई लावै।
सोइ अमित जीवन फल पावै॥**

Whoever approaches You with any wish gets blessed with its fulfilment that stays till eternity.

The third quarter is all about wish-fulfilment. Hanuman grants everything that a devotee can ask for. And Tulsidas says that He can grant still more – the attainment of the highest goal from which there is no return. We know it by different names, depending on the path we have chosen to take. It could be *mukti* for a *bhakta*, *moksha* for a *jnani* and *kaivalya* for a *yogi*. And when we talk of the realization of these goals, we know that they last till eternity.

Amita jeevana phala has been interpreted as getting something which lasts throughout life or lasts for innumerable lifetimes. While the first one is taken in the material sense, attaining the ultimate goal in the spiritual realm is believed to last until eternity.

29. चारों जुग परताप तुम्हारा।
है परसिद्ध जगत उजियारा॥

Your valour prevails in all the four yugas. The glory of Your fame illuminates the whole universe.

The *Mahaviri Vyakhya* argues that the incarnation of Prabhu Rama happened in the twenty-fourth *Treta Yuga* in the *Vaivasvata Manvantara*. During that time, Prabhu had blessed Hanuman to stay alive as long as the *Rama Katha* continued on Earth. Four *chaturyugas* have passed since then, and we are currently living in the twenty-eighth *Kali Yuga*. Even today, both *Rama katha* and Anjaneya are very much present with us.

There is no Puranic account of Hanuman in the *Satya yuga*. In the Mahabharata, however, there is mention of Hanuman narrating the details of all the four yugas to Bhima, which included an account of *Satya yuga*. This proves that He was present in some form or other during that time. In the *Dvapara yuga*, we find Him in the Mahabharata. He manifested Himself to Bhima near a Himalayan plantain grove. There were two specific purposes of His appearance there. Bhima was roaming randomly and had unknowingly advanced very close to a no-entry zone. Bhima's well-being was crucial for the Pandava victory. The Vayuputra wanted to warn Bhima against trespassing into an area of immortals, thereby saving him from divine curse.

Moreover, all the major commanders of the Kaurava army were experts in *divyastras* or divine weapons. Even though Lord Krishna was the charioteer, Arjuna needed an extra layer of protection to absorb and neutralize the weapons shot at him. The Pandava brothers, and Arjuna in particular, must have thought about that repeatedly. Hanuman ji wanted to assure Arjuna by sending a message through Bhima that He would be present on his chariot.

In the war, He did not engage in any direct combat. His wild roar was enough to intimidate the enemy soldiers. However, His actual contribution became clear only after the war was over. Arjuna was instructed by Lord Krishna to get down from the chariot. Then, The Lord Himself got down, and Maruti was the last to leave. The chariot had already come under the impact of *Brahmastra,* but it could resist the damage because of the presence of the Devas. As soon as they left, fire engulfed the car and burnt it down to ashes. So, basically, Maruti acted as an insulator for the chariot.

In the *Kali Yuga*, miracles are often attributed to Hanuman. The poet of the *Chalisa* himself was a beneficiary of His kindness. Legends speak of how His grace had saved Goswami ji from prison. The poet had become very famous in his lifetime, and once he was summoned by Akbar, the Mughal emperor, to display some miracles in his court. When Tulsidas did not comply, Akbar ordered his imprisonment in Fatehpur Sikri. It is believed that the *Chalisa* was composed inside the prison. On the fortieth day, a large army of monkeys descended on the city and started creating havoc. The worried emperor realised his mistakes and released Goswami ji with due respect.

A similar episode had also happened with Samarth Ramdas, the guru of Shivaji and one of the greatest devotees of Maruti. During one of the wars with the Marathas, the Mughal army of Aurangzeb attacked the Sajjangarh fort and surrounded it from all sides. Swami Ramdas, who was inside the fort, started praying to his *Ishta Deva*. Again, from nowhere, descended a huge army of monkeys to the rescue of Swamiji. Aurangzeb recognized this as a divine intervention and retreated from the fort.

The Adhyatma Ramayana ends its *Yuddha Kanda with* the episode where Rama and Sita bless Hanuman after their return to Ayodhya. Hanuman expressed His desire to stay on Earth, reciting the name of Prabhu. Prabhu Rama blessed Him that He would continue to stay in this world until the end of the ongoing *kalpa*. He also promised His *sayujya* for Hanuman after the completion of the ongoing *kalpa*.

In this verse, the poet tells us that Anjaneya is timeless; His presence among all of us is always there.

30. साधु संत के तुम रखवारे।
असुर निकंदन राम दुलारे॥

O Beloved of Sri Rama, You are the guardian of sages and saints, and the destroyer of demons.

This verse marks the end of the third quarter of the *Chalisa*. Maruti is very dear to Sri Rama, and this empowers Him to grant anything a devotee asks for. He can cure diseases and pain, mitigate crises and dispel fear of all kinds, provided three conditions are met. First, the chanting of His name should be uninterrupted (*nirantara japa)*. Secondly, the entire focus of our thoughts, actions and speech should be on Him only (*dhyana* through *mana, karma* and *vachana).* And, finally, we must be honest and truthful (*sadhu–sant*) in our daily lives.

Swami Rambhadracharya ji interprets *sadhu* as one who is on the path of *sadhana,* and uses the term *sant* for the accomplished ones. Hanuman ji is the saviour of both *sadhu* Sugreeva and *sant* Vibhishana.

ॐ

SECTION V

Verses 31 to 40 & The Concluding Doha

The fourth quarter concentrates mainly on how Hanuman ji holds the key to Sri Rama's blessings.

31. अष्ट सिद्धि नौ निधि के दाता।
अस बर दीन जानकी माता॥

Ma Sita blessed You to be the bestower of the eight siddhis and nine nidhis.

This is a unique verse in that it talks about the blessings of Sita Ma on Hanuman ji. All the versions of the Ramayana agree that Maruti was blessed by Her. There are three such occasions where it is believed to have happened: during Her first meeting with Him in Ashoka Garden, at the conclusion of Rama's coronation ceremony, and before Her departure to the supreme abode.

In the Ashoka *Vanika*, Janaki blessed Him with strength, humility, virtues, and freedom from old age and death. Hanuman bowed respectfully and said, "O Mother, I am grateful. Your blessings are very famous and infallible". Valmiki's description is a bit different. Sita did not grant Him any boons directly. Instead, She kindled a fire and prayed to Agni Deva for Anjaneya's immunity from fire during *Lanka dahana* - शीतो भव हनूमतः. As per another legend, Sita blessed Hanuman with immortality just before Her departure to the *parama dhama*. However, these descriptions have no specific reference to the *Siddhi* and *Nidhi*.

Siddhi is a concept of accomplishment prevalent across various sub-branches of the Sanatan tradition, such as Samkhya, Yoga, Tantra, Bhakti and even Ayurveda. It mostly refers to the attainment of supra-human capabilities. Ganesh ji, Hanuman ji and Devi Durga are commonly worshipped as the bestowers of *siddhis*.

The idea of *siddhi* probably originated in the system of Yoga. The *Patanjali Yoga Sutra* describes *siddhi* as the enhancement of the sensory faculties of hearing, feeling (touch), seeing, tasting and smelling. It is variously interpreted by the commentators as the ability to see or hear from a distance, having the perception of the divine taste or smell, and so on.

As per the *Yoga Sutra*, a person can be a *born siddha* or obtain it by using herbs, chanting a mantra, doing *tapasya,* or by attaining *samadhi*. Even without all these, an inner illumination, called *Pratibha* in yogic parlance, can make someone a *siddha*. The most interesting remark of Patanjali on these enhanced capabilities comes as a mild warning! *Siddhi* is a natural by-product of *samadhi*, but *siddhi* per se should not be the goal of a yogi. Instead, *siddhis* are to be considered obstacles in attaining *samadhi*.

Let us come to the more popular aspect of the concept of *siddhi*. The famous *Ashta siddhi,* or the eight accomplishments, have been narrated as *Anima, Mahima, Laghima, Garima, Prapti, Prakamya, Ishitva* and *Vashitva*. Translated into simple English, they mean the ability to make oneself very small (*anima*) or very large (*mahima*), very light (*laghima*) or very heavy (*garima*), the ability to fulfil desire (*prapti*), to have the freedom from desire or making oneself irresistible to others (*prakamya*), having lordship over others (*ishitva*) and the ability to stay unaffected by the three *gunas* (*vashitva*).

This list is found in many of the Puranas with some minor variations. However, the *Bhagavata Purana* speaks of eight major, ten minor, and even five additional *siddhis*. Surprisingly, the major list does not include *garima*; rather, it speaks of *Kamavasayita* or the ability to enjoy the absolute bliss. The major *siddhis* originate directly from the Supreme Lord, whereas the *Prakriti,* with its *Gunas,* is the source of the ten minor ones.

And how are these *siddhis* obtained? In the *Bhagavata Purana*, Lord Krishna says that He, being the Universal Purusha, has multiple aspects. A devotee obtains *siddhis* as per his choice by meditating upon (*dharana*) the specific aspects of the Lord. For example, a *sadhaka* meditating upon the subtleness or *tanmatra* of Him will be blessed with *anima,* and he who contemplates upon the *Mahat tattva* will attain *mahima,* and so on.

The yogic and puranic background of *siddhi* is essential for understanding the Hanuman Chalisa, more specifically, to figure out how Hanuman ji confers these *siddhis* on His devotees. Out of all the methods enumerated in the *Patanjali Yoga Sutra*, Hanuman can bless us with a sacred *mantra*, inspire us to carry on with our *tapasya*, lead us to a state of *samadhi,* or can grant the whole of it in a fraction of a second by illuminating our inner self. The *Bhagavata Purana*, however, mentions only one way: the path of meditation. Anjaneya not only blesses us with the resolve to meditate, but He also guards us against all negative forces throughout the journey.

Though the concept of *Nava Nidhi* or "the nine treasures" is recurrent in our scriptures, there is little clarity about their actual nature. They have been enumerated as *Padma, Mahapadma, Nila, Shankha*, *Kachhapa, Makara, Mukunda*, *Nanda* and *Kharva*. The very famous *Rudra Ashtadhyayi* in the Shukla Yajurveda begins with an address to Ganapati as *Nidhipati*. As per the Mahabharata, *Shankha* and *Padma* are the principal nidhis, though all nine stay in a tangible form in the court of Lord Kuvera.

Nidhis have been commonly interpreted as precious objects. *Nila* could be a blue gemstone, *shankha* a precious conch shell, *kachhapa* and *makara* may mean precious artifacts made from the tortoise shell or crocodile skin, *Mukunda* is cinnabar – a form of mercury ore considered priceless in many ancient cultures, and *kharva* could signify the musk-rose flower. An alternate approach, which sounds more scientific, interprets the *nidhis* as "large numbers" in the counting system of ancient India. Out of the *nava nidhis*, at least five have been used as large numbers- *padma, mahapadma, nila*, *shanka* and *kharva*. And, *kharva* or *kharav* is used even today!

Interestingly, five out of the nine *nidhis* are sourced from water, while two are mined from the Earth. The texts may vary in their interpretations, but one thing is for sure –*nidhis* do not necessarily relate to material wealth.

All these had been bestowed upon our Hanuman ji by Ma Janaki. But why?

By the time Hanuman met Sita, He had already demonstrated some of these *siddhis*. He had resorted to *anima* and *mahima* while engaging with Surasa, Simhika and Lanka Devi! To tell the truth, He had such abilities since His infancy! And He lives a very simple life, so the vast treasures of Kuvera are of no value to Him.

Well, Janaki Mata did not bless Maruti with the eight *siddhis* and nine *nidhis* as He already possessed them. She made Him a **dātā** or a designated **bestower** of these powers and treasures.

32. राम रसायन तुम्हरे पासा ।
सदा रहो रघुपति के दासा ॥

You possess the elixir of devotion to Rama and eternally stay in His service.

The word *Rasayana* is commonly used in the context of an elixir or tonic that promotes wellness, increases vitality and fights infections. For a very long time, mercury or *rasa* dominated the fields of Indian medicine, and *rasayana* stood for mercury-based drugs.

In the realm of spiritualism, *Rama Nama* and *Rama Bhakti* have been considered life-saving elixirs.

Hanuman is not only the custodian of the priceless potion, He Himself is its most prominent user!

Interestingly, *rasayana* has another connotation that relates to the field of alchemy, metallurgy and applied chemistry.

Indian literature acknowledges that Ravana was a great scholar of his time. The very famous *Shiva Tandava Stotra* is attributed to him. He was also believed to be an authority on pharmaceutical chemistry. *Arka Prakasha* is a thousand-verse composition dealing with the pharmacology of ayurvedic drugs; it also deals with rakshasa-related concepts like *vashikarana* and *adrishyakarana*. Some of his contributions to Indian traditional medicine include formulations such as *Madanananda Modaka, Pratapa Lankesvara, Lankesvara Rasa and Lankaadhipesvara Rasa*.

However, relatively less known is the fact that Sri Rama was even a greater scholar than Ravana in the field of applied chemistry. Whereas Ravana chose the field of drug manufacturing, Rama contributed mainly to metallurgy. Bhudev Mookerjee, author of *Rasa Jala Nidhi*, describes Rama as "the brightest luminary in the sky of Indian alchemy". During His long exile in the Dandaka Forest, He learnt the science of *Rasayana* from two scientist-yogis, namely Kalanatha and Lakshmisvara. Two brilliant works in the field of alchemy, *Rasendra Chintamani* and *Ramarajiya*, are ascribed to Sri Rama. A reader of the first book can find methods to prepare nine different kinds of iron in that ancient text. *Ramarajiya* contains a specific reference to the author as the King of Ayodhya who made an idol of His wife in gold, all by Himself.

While all these are speculations in the absence of any historical data, the archaic language of the books and the fact that they have not borrowed anything from or referred to any of the existing texts on the subject establish them as very ancient works for sure. From a very early period, Indians had earned the expertise to make stainless steel, and Sri Rama could have picked up the art from Dandakaranya.

And it would not be unjustified to speculate that Sri Rama would have entrusted all this knowledge to His closest associate, Hanuman, who continued to be the custodian of that treasure.

The road to Rama passes through Hanuman. One has to worship the Vayuputra as He only holds the elixir of devotion to the Supreme Lord.

33. तुम्हरे भजन राम को पावै।
जनम जनम के दुख बिसरावै॥

34. अन्त काल रघुबरपुर जाई।
जहां जन्म हरिभक्त कहाई॥

One who sings Your praise, finds Rama and gets liberated from the sufferings of several lifetimes.

After death, he attains the Abode of Rama and stays a devotee of The Lord even if he is reborn.

Verse 32 of the last *chaupai* and both the verses of this *chaupai* (verses 33 and 34) refer to the oneness of Hanuman ji and Sri Rama.

One needs to recognize that the elixir of *Rama Bhakti* stays in the custody of Maruti. His grace is essential to have devotion towards Raghupati. Prayers to Him, in fact, reach Rama, and the devotee gets rid of the sufferings of countless lifetimes. When such a devotee dies, he attains the *parama dhama* of Sri Rama. Exercising his free will, he can choose to be born again. The famous tag of being Rama's devotee always stays with him even if he comes back to the world.

Rama's *Rasayana* is such a potent elixir that whoever tastes it once becomes endowed with *Hari bhakti* for multiple lifetimes.

The *Chalisa* is a text of integration. It integrates the various philosophies prevalent among the *bhakti* sects. A devotee, depending upon the path of sadhana, may seek *moksha* or *punarjanma*. The text of the *Chalisa* assures us that there is no place for disappointment in Hanuman worship. The devotee gets *moksha* through *bhakti* and attains the supreme abode of the *Brahman*. But he can choose to be in the eternal service of the Lord or enjoy the elixir of *bhakti* in the human form.

35. और देवता चित्त न धरई।
हनुमत सेइ सर्बसुख करई॥

One need not pray to any other God; happiness of all kinds can be attained through Hanumanji's blessings.

There is nothing that Anjaneya cannot grant – wealth, knowledge, devotion, physical strength, good health, supernatural powers, a permanent seat in Prabhu Rama's abode, and whatnot!

Anjaneya is unique in the Sanatan pantheon in the sense that He is related to so many Devas and Devis. The legends of His origin relate Him to Lord Shiva and Vayu Deva. He draws all His power from His absolute devotion to Sri Rama. Ma Sita, an *avatara* of Lakshmi Devi, has blessed Him with strength, virtues and immortality. He accompanies Devi Durga during Her march. Lord Brahma, Indra Deva and other major Gods have infused their own strength and greatness into Him.

Surya Deva, who illuminates all from within and outside, is His teacher.

The entire divinity is at play through Hanuman, as He was cut out to be a protective and benevolent God for eternity. And, in fact, He is!

There is absolute freedom in our tradition to worship any Deva or Devi as per our liking and need. And all of us pray the same Supreme *Brahman* in different *rupas*. Tulsidas eulogizes Sri Hanuman as the one-stop solution for all our material and spiritual needs.

36. संकट कटै मिटै सब पीरा।
जो सुमिरै हनुमत बलबीरा॥

He who recalls the Mighty Hanuman gets rid of all his difficulties and sufferings.

Anjaneya is revered as *Sankat Mochan* across India and even beyond. This image of Him as a crisis manager or a protector from crisis is a recurrent one in the Ramayana. The epic is full of descriptions of how He acted as the saviour during difficult times.

Suffering could be due to a divine curse; it can have its origin in the physical environment, or it could even be due to our own fault. It can affect our material life or our spiritual progress. The source from which it comes and the level at which it affects do not matter as long as we recall Hanuman ji.

He lives among us and listens to our prayers. On a more subtle level, He is the one who can grant absolute bliss and complete freedom from spiritual obstacles.

37. जय जय जय हनुमान गोसाईं।
कृपा करहु गुरुदेव की नाईं॥

Glory be to You, O Hanuman ji, my master. Bless me just as my Guru would do.

Goswami is someone whose senses are absolutely under his control, and it seems more than appropriate to address Hanuman ji as *Goswami*. It is a Vaishnava tradition, and the title started with Ugrashravas Sauti, also known as Suta Goswami, the third composer of the Mahabharata.

Interestingly, the first *chaupai* of the *Chalisa* mentions the term "Jaya" twice. Translated into simple English, *jaya* means *victory* or *glory to* someone. When Tulsidas reaches almost the end of the *Chalisa*, he uses the expression three times in succession. This "triple glory" is a poetic style commonly adopted while composing spiritual songs. In a subliminal sense, *Jaya,* at the beginning, is for an ocean of knowledge and good qualities, and *Jaya* once more is for the king of *Vanaras,* who illuminates the three worlds. Now, towards the end of the *Chalisa*, *Jaya* has tripled for a *Guru* and *Goswami*!

Tulsidas seeks *kripa* from Sri Hanuman the way he would seek it from his own Guru. The Devas do bless us, but they can be a little strict and harsh, if need be. But a guru is full of kindness, and he is all forgiving. The essence of *kripa karahu Gurudeva ki nai* can be summarized as: "O Prabhu Hanuman, please be like my human guru. I seek your forgiveness beforehand. I expect pure kindness and nothing else from You!"

38. जो शत बार पाठ कर कोई।
छूटहिं बंदि महा सुख होई॥

Whoever recites the Hanuman Chalisa one hundred times gets liberated from bondages and attains great happiness.

This verse and the subsequent one are part of the *phalashruti* of the Hanuman Chalisa. Most spiritual texts have a proclamation towards the end that enumerates the benefits of reading or listening to them.

The composer has enlisted three major benefits for the reader of the verses: he will be free of bondage, attain great happiness, and have *siddhi* or accomplishments. All three merits can have multiple connotations.

Bondage can be material, such as financial burdens and diseases. It can be mental and spiritual, where our ego and a lack of divine intervention appear as obstacles in our path to self-realization. Similarly, *maha sukha* cannot just be worldly pleasures; it should have a higher meaning, such as unwavering devotion or an uninterrupted divine experience. It could also mean the attainment of the *parama dhama* of the *Prabhu*.

And *shata* is probably suggestive of a daily practice for a long time rather than the exact repetition of one hundred times.

Jo koi is part of a promise that these merits will accrue to all sincere reciters of the *Chalisa*, without preconditions.

39. जो यह पढ़ै हनुमान चलीसा।
होय सिद्धि साखी गौरीसा॥

Whoever recites this Hanuman Chalisa obtains accomplishments for sure. Mahadeva, The Lord of Gauri, is witness to this.

This verse is also a part of the *phalashruti* and carries the same essence as the previous one.

The positioning of *"Jo"* at the beginning of the verse is all about democratizing the benefits of devotion to the entire humanity - *Hanuman Chalisa* is for everyone. Both the mentions of *Jo* in the present and the previous verse are probably a reflection of Goswamiji's *Ramanandi* root. Sant Ramanand, the founder of the sect, had famously said, "Do not inquire about the caste and community of a devotee. Whoever prays to God surely belongs to Him." (जाति-पाति पूछे नहीं कोई, हरि को भजे सो हरि के होई)

The second half of the verse is very thought-provoking.

Tulsidas has composed the *Ramcharitmanas* as a conversation between Devi Uma and Mahadeva. And now he invokes the Lord to conclude the Hanuman Chalisa. Keeping Gaurisha in the verse may seem to be a formality, just a poetic style of composing a *phalashruti* verse. But the poet knew in his heart of hearts that it was Mahadeva's blessing that was working through him during the composition of the *Chalisa*.

Ma Sita had blessed Hanuman to become a bestower of *Siddhis*. And it is natural that one who recites the Hanuman *Chalisa*, otherwise named as the *Vimala Yasha* of His Master *Raghuvara*, would attain those *siddhis*.

And to this proclamation, Mahadeva, the Lord of the Universe and the Lord of Gauri Devi, is the guarantor.

Sanatana tradition stands tall even today because its sects have always chosen to respect and assimilate contrasting views. No one has mastered this art better than Tulsidas, who has united both the Lords Vishnu and Mahadeva in all his compilations. Composing verses in Hanumanji's honour and styling it as the praise song of His master Sri Rama, mentioning that Hanuman ji became a bestower of *siddhis* to His devotees through Ma Sita's blessings, and concluding that those *siddhis* could be attained by any ordinary reciter of these verses under Mahadeva's guarantee – such an extraordinary effort can be expected only from a saint of Goswamiji's calibre.

40. तुलसीदास सदा हरि-चेरा ।
कीजै नाथ हृदय महँ डेरा ॥

Tulsidas, the eternal servant of Sri Hari, prays,
"O Lord Hanuman, please stay in my heart".

Like many other verses in the *Chalisa*, this one is also associated with multiple interpretations. The poet claims himself to be an eternal servant of Sri Hari and urges Maruti to reside within his heart. This seems logical because Maruti listens to those who invoke the name of His Master, Sri Hari. In a way, Tulsidas is narrating his qualifications before urging Hanuman to bless him.

But then again, Hari is a synonym of *Vanara,* and *Hari-chera* can be interpreted as a servant of Hanuman. In other words, a devotee with *dasya bhava* is urging his Master to have His abode within him.

Given the fact that the poet has already used the word Hari in the *Chalisa* with the meaning of Sri Rama, the first of the interpretations seems more appropriate.

Tulsidas has come to the conclusion. Absolute happiness, supernatural powers, wealth, devotion, successful passage through times of crisis, freedom from diseases and sufferings, freedom from fear of evil spirits; everything a mortal can comprehend has been asked for.

Now, the time has come to speak out the ultimate desire– requesting Hanuman ji to stay within our hearts. This feeling is reinforced in the concluding Doha; the longing and demand increase further. It now includes the Family – Sri Rama, Lakshmana, and Sita Ma, along with Hanuman ji.

पवनतनय संकटहरन मंगलमूरति रूप।
राम लखन सीता सहित हृदय बसहु सुरभूप॥

O Son of the Wind God, You are the remover of obstacles, the embodiment of auspiciousness, and the king of Gods. Please stay in my heart along with Rama, Lakshmana and Sita.

The previous verse has a continuity of sense with the concluding *doha*. Though literally implicit, the words almost reveal what Goswami ji wants to say in these two verses, "O Hanuman ji, king of Devas, I invoke your auspicious form. I have a longing for so many lifetimes that You, along with Sita Ma, Sri Rama and Sri Lakshmana, would bless me eternally with Your holy presence within me. I aspire for this alone, but the hardships and confusions of life keep disturbing me. Please take care of the obstacles on my path. O Lords, let my mind-heart-soul, my entire existence, be Your permanent abode. Let my individual identity merge with Your Supreme Being."

The outline of the spiritual protocol was laid down at the very beginning of the *Chalisa*. The primary objective was to prepare this earthly body, along with its mind and senses, to be an abode of divinity.

The process started with cleansing the mind through the blessings of the Guru. Pain and deformities were taken care of by Hanuman's blessings. Focus of the entire being was set upon Him, and this prepared the mind to receive the light of the soul. *Avichala Bhakti* to Hanuman brought the presence of Rama, Lakshmana and Sita into the soul. Hanuman ji also came to reside there in His most auspicious form. Now, the devotee's self-realisation is complete when his individual existence has been taken over by the Supreme Soul. He realizes the essential oneness and non-duality between him and the *Parama Purusha*. The follower of Samkhya gets his *moksha*, the Yogi gets his *kaivalya,* and the *Bhakta* gets his *sayujya* with The Divine.

Hanuman ji is immortal, and so are the merits of reciting His glory. This makes the text of the Hanuman Chalisa timeless!

ॐ